Climbing with Jesus

Climbing with Jesus

A Fresh Look at the Sermon on the Mount

STEPHEN GRUNLAN

RESOURCE *Publications* · Eugene, Oregon

CLIMBING WITH JESUS
A Fresh Look at the Sermon on the Mount

Resource Publications
An Imprint of Wipf and Stock Publishers
199 W. 8th Ave., Suite 3
Eugene, OR 97401
www.wipfandstock.com

ISBN 13: 978-1-60899-037-5

Manufactured in the U.S.A.

To the people of Osage Alliance Church
who are climbing with Jesus

Contents

Introduction

THIS BOOK GREW OUT of a sermon series I preached on the Sermon on the Mount. That sermon series resulted from an extended study of the Gospels. I wanted to study the life of Jesus. I read through the Gospels in as many different translations of the New Testament as I could locate. As I did I cataloged the characteristics of Jesus. Looking back I realize that Jesus lived out what he taught in the Sermon of the Mount.

I also began to see the Sermon on the Mount as the manifesto of his Kingdom. Not a future kingdom, but his present kingdom. Satan is the ruler of this world. The Bible tells us he is the prince of this world (John 12:31; 14:30 16:11), the prince of the power of the air (Ephesians 2:2), and a king (Revelation 9:11). This world is enemy territory. As Jesus told Pilate, his kingdom is not of this world (John 18:36).

As believers we represent Christ's kingdom and are to live out its values. The Sermon on the Mount lays out the values of Christ's kingdom. It is in living out these values that we can subvert the kingdom of this world. We are revolutionaries inside the enemy's kingdom. But our revolution is not one of violence and force. It is a revolution of love and peace based on obedience to our Lord and living out his values.

It is my prayer that this book will help you take a fresh look at Jesus' manifesto and provide practical application for carrying it out. It is my hope you will read the biblical text before reading each chapter and that you will keep your Bible open as you read. May the words of our Lord Jesus Christ penetrate your heart and mind and find expression in your life.

Climbing with Jesus

Matthew 5:1–2

THERE IS A STORY told by Native Americans about a brave who found an eagle's egg. He placed the egg in the nest of a prairie chicken. The eaglet hatched with the brood of chicks and grew up with them. All his life, thinking he was a prairie chicken, the eagle did what prairie chickens do. He scratched in the dirt for seeds and insects to eat. He clucked and cackled in an odd sort of way. He flew in brief flurries of thrashing wings never rising more than a few feet above the ground. After all, that is how prairie chickens fly.

Years passed and the eagle grew older. One day he saw a magnificent bird far above him in the cloudless sky gracefully soaring on powerful wings. "What a beautiful bird," the eagle said to a prairie chicken, "what is it?"

"That's an eagle, the king of birds," replied the prairie chicken, "but don't give it a thought, you can never be like him." And the eagle never gave it a second thought; he went back to scratching in the dirt for seeds and insects. And, eventually the eagle died believing he was a prairie chicken.

How tragic, the eagle was created to fly gracefully on powerful wings in the heavens. But instead it spent its entire life scratching in the dirt. However what is even more tragic is that people God created in his image, created to be full of grace and power, live their lives scratching in the dirt for existence and momentary pleasures. God created us and redeemed us to soar to spiritual heights. God sent his Son to die for us so we could be released from sin and know God's grace and power in our lives.

In the first two verses of Matthew, chapter 5, as set forth in *The Message*, we read, "When Jesus saw his ministry drawing huge crowds, he climbed a hillside. Those who were apprenticed to him, the committed, climbed with him." The question each of us faces is: are we going to climb with Jesus or are we going to stay down with the crowds? In Matthew, chapters 5, 6, and 7, we find climbing instructions in what is known as the Sermon on the Mount.

In order for us to fully understand the Sermon on the Mount we need to see the background or setting for Jesus' message. Verses 1 and 2 set the stage for the sermon. Both Matthew and Luke place the Sermon on the Mount very early in Jesus' ministry, shortly after selecting his disciples. In Matthew 4:18–20 we find Jesus calling his disciples and then, in chapter 5, we find the Sermon on the Mount. In Luke 6:12–19, we find Jesus calling his disciples and then in verse 20 he begins the Sermon on the Mount. Luke records an abbreviated version of the sermon while Matthew gives us the whole message.

Toward the end of Matthew, chapter 4, we see that crowds had begun to follow Jesus. Then in verse 23 we see they followed him from town to town. Now in verse 1 of chapter 5 we find Jesus attempting to get away from the crowds to be alone with his disciples. Matthew tells us he sat down.

When a Jewish rabbi taught his disciples he would sit with them gathered around him. Jesus went up on a mountainside and gathered his disciples around him. While some of the crowd apparently followed and listened in, Jesus was addressing his disciples. In fact Luke does not even mention the crowds, only the disciples. Luke 6:20 tells us, "And turning his gaze on his disciples he began to say. . . ." The Sermon on the Mount is a message for Christ's disciples. The Sermon on the Mount is not a message for the world or the lost, it is a message for the followers of Jesus, for those who want to climb with him.

After delivering a carefully prepared sermon a guest speaker stood at the door with the pastor to greet the people. There he received compliments on his sermon as the parishioners filed out. It was the sort of ritual that occurs each week in many churches. The people thanked the speaker for being there and expressed appreciation for his message.

That is, all except one man. When he reached the speaker he said, "That was a terrible sermon." Although he was taken back, the speaker maintained his composure. The man got back in line and came through a second time and said to the speaker, "Your stories were dull and boring." Then he came through a third time and said, "Your message made no sense."

By now the host pastor was thoroughly embarrassed and tried to rectify the situation. He whispered to the guest speaker, "Don't pay any attention to him. He's not very smart. He can't think for himself. In fact all he does is just repeats what he hears everyone else saying."

That is almost as bad as the woman who came up to her pastor after a service and enthusiastically gushed, "Oh Pastor, your sermons are such a blessing, why each one is better than the next one." Or the man who told his pastor, "Your sermons are like water to a drowning man."

In Matthew 7:28 we find the reaction of those who heard Jesus sermon, it says, "they were amazed at his teaching." The Greek sword translated *amazed* is strong word that could be translated astonished. Why was there such a striking reaction to Jesus' message? In Matthew 7:29 we are told, "He taught as one who had authority and not as the teachers of the law."

A tradition had built up around the Law in the Judaism of Jesus' day. The scribes and the Pharisees paid lip service to the law but their real loyalty was to their traditions. When the rabbis taught, they would never initiate any teaching on their own authority, or even the authority of the Word of God. Rather they taught rabbinical traditions by quoting famous rabbis. But Jesus' teaching was different. Jesus taught with his own authority and the authority of the Word of God. Jesus did not say, "As rabbi so-and-so has written. . . . ." Rather Jesus proclaimed, "I say to you . . ." or "The Scriptures say. . . ."

Jesus' message was a revolutionary one based on relationships not religion, first a relationship with God and then a relationship with others. Jesus declared the religious establishment of his day bankrupt. He had no use for religion. His message was a revolutionary one based on relationships. The whole Sermon on the Mount deals with our relationship with God and our relationships with each other. It calls for radical change in how we relate to God and how we relate to each other. If we would implement it we could impact our world. It is the manifesto of a new kingdom, one that will take over this world. A message that amazed people some 2,000 years ago is equally amazing today.

In fact, the Sermon on the Mount is so revolutionary that many students of the Bible have sought to dismiss it. Some have taught it is an ideal that is not attainable. Others have argued it does not apply to believers today. They say it refers to the Millennium when Jesus will return to set up his earthly kingdom. Others claim it applied only to the interim period between the Law and the gospel.

However I believe it applied to Jesus' followers in his day and I believe it applies to Jesus' followers today. In the Sermon on the Mount Jesus speaks of persecution, enemies, evil and other things that will not be present in the Millennium. And, except when he refers to the Law, all the verbs Jesus uses are in the Greek present tense which indicates a present and ongoing action.

I believe the Sermon on the Mount is God's message for us today. I believe God wants us to be kingdom people bringing his revolution into a world ruled by Satan. I believe God wants us to be revolutionaries in enemy territory introducing his kingdom in this world. I believe God is calling us to impact our community and our world with the message of Jesus Christ. I believe we are called to be part of a counter-cultural movement.

A lot of communities have Little League or Pop Warner football programs for children. In a Midwestern community a man walked into the recreation department a week before the football season was to begin. He asked if any of the football teams needed a coach. He was told there was one team left, but all the other teams had already chosen their players. All that was left were the runts and the misfits no one else wanted. The man said that would be fine.

So he took the runts and the misfits and began to work with them. It was only a week until the first game so he knew he could not teach them much. The running backs knew how to run up the middle so all week long he worked on blocking. At the game that week it did not take the other team long to figure out his one play and stop the runts and misfits. But the other team could not score on their defense and the game ended in a scoreless tie.

All the next week the team of runts and misfits worked on blocking and running left. The next week they won their game because they scored a touchdown. The third week the team of runts and misfits worked on running right. Now they had three plays. They could run left, run right, and run up the middle. That week they lost, but they did score two touchdowns.

During the fourth week the coach had to be out of town on business and he asked some of the fathers to take over. The fathers had been frustrated with the coach's simple game plan so they introduced one of their own. The coach arrived back in town the day of the game and drove straight to the field. It was the end of the first quarter, the score was 21 to zero in favor of the other team. Everyone was running in a different direction. Seven kids went out for a pass and nobody blocked. The kids were confused and crying.

So the coach called a timeout and pulled them together and asked what was wrong. They said, "We can't remember 42 sweep and 23 fly and 51 dive." The coach said reassuringly, "That's okay, we'll use, go left and go right and go up the middle and block. Keep it simple." The boys returned to the field. They ran left and they ran right and they ran up the middle and they blocked. They kept it simple and kept the other team from scoring again and even scored twice themselves.

The fathers who had been left in charge started to protest until one of them noticed something. The coach who had taught the boys only three plays was wearing a Superbowl ring. Then they realized the coach knew 42 sweep, 51 dive, 23 fly, and whole bunch of other plays. But he also knew the kids and their limitations and he knew he had to keep it simple.

In the Sermon on the Mount Jesus has kept it simple for us. The message is stated in simple terms and is so clearly articulated anyone can grasp what Jesus is saying. Yet as simple as the message is, it is a difficult one to follow. Jesus invites us to climb with him.

As we seek to apply what we have learned, we will look at what it takes to climb with Jesus. First, climbing with Jesus takes sacrifice. In Mark 8:34 Jesus Christ declared, "If anyone would come after me, they must deny themselves and take up their cross and follow me."

We cannot spend Sunday mornings in recreational activities and be in church worshipping God. We cannot read the latest best-seller and study God's Word at the same time. We cannot watch television in the evening and minister with children or students. We cannot buy everything we want and still support God's work. Now there is nothing wrong with recreation, best sellers, shopping, or television. However, we have to give up some things for other things. If we want to climb with Jesus we have to give up the things that keep us from climbing.

One Olympic sport where Americans always do well is competitive swimming. Many Olympians are college students. Do you know what many of them do the year they are going to compete in the Olympics? They drop out of school for the year and they spend 6 hours a day in training and conditioning. They set aside anything and everything that will interfere with their goal of winning a gold medal. The Bible, in Hebrews

12:1, tells us to set aside every weight and hindrance that keeps us from following Jesus. Each of us needs to ask ourselves: what is keeping me from climbing with Jesus?

Second, climbing with Jesus takes commitment. Jesus did not just say to deny ourselves, he also said we were to take up our crosses and follow him. Many people think crosses are things that happen to them. But crosses do not happen to us, we need to take them up. Following Jesus is a choice. We need to ask ourselves: have I chosen to climb with Jesus?

Third, climbing with Jesus takes effort. Climbing is not easy. Someone has said, "The road to success is uphill all the way." We need to ask ourselves: am I willing to put in the effort to climb with Jesus? While climbing with Jesus takes sacrifice, commitment and effort, climbing with Jesus is worth it.

A trapper had been out in the wilderness for months running his trap lines. Now it was time to come to town to sell his furs. When he arrived at the fur-trader's store he saw a beautiful bald eagle perched on the stand it was chained to. After selling his furs the trapper asked the trader how much he wanted for the eagle. The trader asked a price equal to almost half what the trader had sold his furs for.

Without batting an eye the trapper paid the trader. Then he walked over to the perch, unchained the eagle, put it on his arm and walked out. The eagle remained calmly perched on the trapper's arm as he walked down the main street. It made no attempt to fly off. When they came to the end of Main Street, the sun hit the eagle's eye and it looked toward the snow-capped mountains in the distance. Then the eagle spread its mighty wings, shrieked, and took off. As it soared into the sky the trapper smiled.

How is it with you? Jesus paid for our salvation with his life. Now he asks us to climb with him. What will it be? Will I continue to scratch in the dirt with the crowd like the eagle raised with the prairie chickens, or will I soar with Jesus like the eagle set free by the trapper? We have two options for dealing with this invitation to climb with Jesus. One option is to ignore it. The other option is to accept Jesus' invitation to climb with him. The choice is ours, scratch or soar. I do not know about you, but I want to soar.

2

How to Be Happy

Matthew 5:3–12

ONE SUNDAY MORNING A young woman entered the single adults' Sunday School class with a great big smile. She began to pass out blue lollipops as she explained, "It's a boy." The class began to become uneasy as this single and heretofore very proper young woman expressed her happiness. Then she declared, "It's a boy! Six foot one, 180 pounds," as she showed off her engagement ring. The young lady was obviously happy. But would she be just as happy six months after she was married? Six years later? We all want to be happy. What is the secret of happiness? We find it in Matthew 5:3–12.

In this chapter we will be studying the opening section of the Sermon on the Mount known as the beatitudes. I will confess that I considered writing a separate chapter on each of the beatitudes. However I have come to the conclusion that the beatitudes are a unit and are best dealt with as such.

Each of the beatitudes calls those who do certain things blessed and then explains why. Before we look at the beatitudes we need to understand what the word *blessed* means. There are actually two Greek words used in the New Testament that are translated *blessed*. One means "to speak well of." But that is not the word used here. The Amplified Bible translates the Greek word used here, "enjoying enviable happiness." The Phillips translation begins each of the beatitudes with, "How happy are. . . ."

In the Greek text, the language in which the New Testament was originally written, the Greek word translated *blessed* is in the plural and is literally translated "happinesses." The concept conveyed is that of great happiness. However, it is not a happiness based on circumstances rather it is a happiness based on our attitudes and actions. Happiness based on circumstances such as getting engaged are subject to what happens to us and are out of our control. If something good happens we are happy, if something bad happens we are not happy. But happiness based on our attitudes and actions is within our control so we control our happiness. Life is not what happens to us. Life is how we respond to what happens to us.

Now remember what we have already learned. Jesus is addressing his followers, his disciples, those who want to climb with him. This control of our attitudes and actions is not possible without supernatural help. Humanly speaking no one can pull it off, but we are not talking humanly we are talking supernaturally. Jesus Christ is in the happiness business. Now you might not believe that by looking at some of his followers.

It was Friday evening and three couples decided to go to a local steak house for some food and fellowship. When they arrived the hostess took their names and said there would be a wait for a table. They were ushered into a crowded, noisy room and told to wait until their name was called. As they waited a waitress came by and said, "Welcome to happy hour, would you like a drink?" The three couples graciously declined.

A few minutes later another waitress came by and said, "Welcome to happy hour, would you like a drink?" Again they declined.

One of the men said to the group, "They probably just make us wait in here hoping to sell us drinks."

Just then another waitress came by and said, "Welcome to happy hour. . . ." Before she could ask if they wanted drinks, one of the wives said, "Listen, we go to First Church and this is as happy as we get. So please tell them to get our table ready."

The Lord wants people who attend First Church and all his people to be happy. Jesus is in the happiness business. He wants us to be happy; he wants you to be happy. Jesus wants all his followers to be happy and he began his very first sermon by telling us how to be happy. Now, he is not talking about us finding happiness in our circumstances, he is talking about us finding happiness through our attitudes and actions.

As we look at the beatitudes I will confess I am not always happy. I will confess I do not always practice the attitudes and actions Jesus taught. This message is for me as well as you so we need to learn together how to be happy.

The dominant philosophy in all of human social history has been to grab for all you can get. But Jesus says the truly happy people are poor in spirit. When Jesus talks about being poor in spirit what exactly does he mean? Jesus is not talking about material poverty but spiritual poverty.

In the Greek language there are two words that mean *poor*. One word refers to a person who has to work fulltime to barely scratch out a living. The person is barely able to survive. The other word refers to people so poor they have to beg. They have no resources within themselves to even live, they are totally dependent on the charity of others. It is the second word that is used here.

We find an example of this level of poverty in Luke 16:19–21, where we read, "There was a rich man who was dressed in purple and fine linen and lived in luxury every day. At his gate was laid a beggar named Lazarus, covered with sores and longing to eat what fell from the rich man's table. Even the dogs came and licked his sores."

The truth is, spiritually we are all like Lazarus. None of us has the resources to help ourselves spiritually. Jesus gives us an example of a person who recognizes their spiritual poverty and one who does not in Luke 18:10–14, "Two men went up to the temple to pray, one a Pharisee and the other a tax collector. The Pharisee stood up and prayed . . .'God I thank you that I am not like other men—robbers, evil doers, adulterers—or even like this tax collector. I fast twice a week and give a tenth of all I get.' But the tax collector stood at a distance. He would not even look up to heaven, but beat his breast and said, 'God, have mercy on me, a sinner.' I tell you this man, rather than the other, went home justified before God." Only those who admit their spiritual poverty can inherit the Kingdom of God.

In my theological training I took a course in comparative religions where we studied the world's major religions. I also took a course in modern religious movements where we studied the major cults found in America. In every religion and cult we studied people's salvation was ultimately based on their works. Knowing one's salvation is ultimately based on works leads to anxiety and guilt, and anxiety and guilt, whatever they produce, they do not produce happiness.

In contrast Biblical Christianity recognizes we are all in spiritual poverty and there is nothing we can do to save ourselves. However it also recognizes that when we admit our poverty and come to God in faith, he provides our salvation though his Son, Jesus Christ. Jesus paid the penalty for our sin with his death. It is complete, paid in full.

That leads to a question: Why does spiritual poverty make us happy? Because when we recognize our spiritual poverty then we will turn to God. When we come to God asking him to forgive us because Jesus died for our sins, he forgives us and comes into our lives through the Holy Spirit. Then we inherit the Kingdom of God and enjoy guilt-free living. Our happiness results from our relationship with God. As long as we recognize our spiritual poverty and turn to God we will know happiness.

The next beatitude seems like a contradiction; "Happy are those who mourn. . . ." Whatever we associate with mourning, it is not happiness. Sorrow, grief, and mourning are part and parcel of life. Evidence of this is that there are nine verbs in the Greek language that express grief and all nine are used in the New Testament. The Greek word used here is the strongest of those nine words. It is a word usually reserved for mourning for the dead. It is sometimes translated *wailing*.

The verse does not say, but given the immediate context as well as the biblical context, most New Testament scholars agree it refers to grief over sin. The Bible tells us in Ephesians 4:30 that when we sin we grieve the Holy Spirit. And when we sin we should be grieved. As the bumper sticker says, "Christians aren't perfect, just forgiven." We do fail; we do sin. The question is: what do we do about it?

In Luke 22 we find the Biblical account of Peter denying Jesus following the Lord's arrest. The cock crows and Peter remembers the words of Jesus foretelling his denial. What was Peter's response to the conviction of sin? He did not rationalize. He did not try to justify himself. He did not make excuses. He did not say, "Anyone else would have done the same thing under those circumstances." Rather, Luke 22:62, tells us, "He went outside and wept bitterly."

That leads to a question: why does mourning lead to happiness? Because we will be comforted. Notice Jesus did not say that mourners are blessed or happy because they mourn, but because they are comforted. It is not until we are grieved enough over our sin to acknowledge it and confess it that we can be forgiven and comforted.

A person who claims to be a Christian and can live in continuous sin without being miserable had better reexamine their faith. The Bible teaches that God convicts and disciplines his children. In fact grief over sin is one of the evidences that we are a child of God. If you can sin and not be uncomfortable, you may not be a child of God.

However Christians who grieve over sin and confess it will be forgiven and comforted. The Bible tells believers in 1 John 1:9, "If we confess our sins God is faithful and just to forgive us our sins and to cleanse us from all unrighteousness." Sin may bring short-term pleasure but it brings long-term grief. Happiness comes from dealing with sin and receiving God's forgiveness and comfort.

The world tells us might makes right. The world tells us the toughest will win. But Jesus says happy are the meek for they shall inherit the earth. Back in Genesis 13 we find an interesting story. The parents of a young man named Lot had died and his uncle, Abraham, took him under his wing. Because of his association with Abraham, Lot began to prosper. Soon Lot's herds and Abraham's herds were so large they could not be pastured together.

Abraham could have turned to Lot and said, "God gave me the land. I have the covenant. You take your herds and find your own land." Instead Abraham said to Lot, "There's plenty of land here. You pick the part you want and I'll take the rest."

Lot picked what appeared to be the best part for himself. The world would say Abraham was a sucker and Lot was the smart one. But God was with Abraham. The descendents of Lot were the Moabites and the Amorites; those people no longer exist. The descendents of Abraham were Jacob, David, Jesus, and the modern Jews who possess the land of Israel.

Meekness is not weakness; it is realizing that the Christian life must be lived by the power of the Holy Spirit. That leads to a question: Why are the meek happy? Because, while they realize they cannot do it on their own, they know God's power is available to them. In John 15:15 Jesus said, "Without me you can do nothing." But back in John 14:12–17 Jesus said we would do greater things than he did because he would send the Holy Spirit to help us.

The first three beatitudes speak of our poverty and weakness and inability to produce righteousness ourselves. Food and water are necessary for physical life. Jesus says righteousness is necessary for spiritual life.

Even the constitution of our country speaks of the pursuit of happiness. The problem is most people look in all the wrong places. Some people think alcohol, drugs, illicit sex, and other activities will make them happy. They may bring momentary pleasure but they do not bring real happiness. Other people think popularity, power, position, or possessions will bring happiness. But some of the most miserable people in the world are the rich and the famous.

And that leads to a question: why will those who hunger and thirst after righteousness be happy? Because they will be satisfied. My wife and I enjoy eating out. We especially enjoy buffets. When we go to a buffet we always feel satisfied. However several hours later we are hungry again. We need to continually eat to stay alive. We cannot eat one big meal and have it last a lifetime. And so it is with hungering and thirsting for righteousness. The verb tense used in this verse indicates a continuous or on-going action. We are continually to be hungry and thirsty for righteousness and we will be continually filled and therefore continually happy.

The fifth beatitude is happy are the merciful. There is a parable Jesus told about a servant who owed his master a large sum of money, the equivalent of several million dollars (the point being it was a debt beyond repayment). The servant asked for mercy and the master forgave the debt. The servant who had been forgiven the huge debt came across another servant who owed him the equivalent of fifty dollars. The servant asked for mercy. But the first servant would not be merciful; he had the servant who owed him $50 thrown into debtors' prison. When the master learned what the first servant, who he had forgiven of a huge debt, had done, he had him thrown into debtors' prison.

The point of the parable and the beatitude is that if we have truly received mercy we will be merciful. The person who is not merciful has not really accepted mercy. Now, God's mercy does not depend on our being merciful, that would be salvation by works. Rather our being merciful is the evidence that we have really received God's mercy. And that leads to a question: why are the merciful happy? Because they have received God's mercy.

Jesus went on to say, "Happy are the pure in heart. . . ." Before we go on, we need to make a point: in the Bible the heart symbolizes the decision-making organ. And that leads to our question: why are the pure in heart happy? Because they will see God. In fact, the Bible teaches you cannot see God unless you are pure in heart. Let me point out a verse you may never have noticed before, Hebrews 12:14. There we read, "Make every effort to live in peace with everyone and to be holy; without holiness no one will see the Lord." Did you catch that last phrase? "Without holiness no one will see God."

Well if we will not see God without holiness or a pure heart, how do we get it? In Psalm 51:10 David prayed, "Create in me a pure heart. . . ." The word translated create is the Hebrew word *bara*. It is the same word that is used in Genesis 1 and it means to create from nothing. Only God can give us a pure heart.

In Ezekiel 36:25–27 God says, "I will cleanse you from all your impurities . . . I will give you a new heart and put in new Spirit in you; I will remove your heart of stone and give you a heart of flesh. And I will put my spirit in you and move you to follow my decrees and be careful to keep my laws."

God's commands and laws are for our benefit; they are given to guide and protect us. The Bible tells us that sin will give us pleasure for a moment but at God's right hand are eternal pleasures. While sin may give pleasure for a moment and obedience may be hard for a moment, sin ultimately pays off in pain and death while obedience pays off in joy and eternal life.

Next Jesus says, "Happy are the peacemakers. . . ." When Jesus was asked what was the greatest commandment he responded, "Love the Lord your God with all your heart, all your soul, and all your mind." Then Jesus added, "The second is like it: Love your neighbor as yourself."

That leads to a question: Who are the peacemakers? Those who have first made their peace with God and then have made their peace with their neighbors. And that leads to a second question: why are the peacemakers happy? Because they will be called the children of God.

Some people claim we are all God's children. That sounds so right, so ecumenical, so inclusive, but it is unbiblical. The Bible says, in John 1:12, "To all who received Jesus, to those who believed in his name, he gave the right to become the children of God." And the Bible tells us in Romans 8:14, "those who are lead by the Spirit are the children of God." The evidence that we are the children of God is that we are peacemakers.

New Testament scholars are divided over whether verses 10 and 11 are two separate beatitudes or a single one. Their debate need not concern us since both verses deal with persecution. Again we come to what seems to be a paradox. You know what a paradox is? It is when a male doctor marries a female doctor and you get a paradox. Seriously, a paradox is something that seems like a contradiction but is true. How can someone be happy when they are being persecuted?

The closing scene of Sholem Asch's classic novel *The Apostle*, takes place in a dungeon in Rome. Hundreds of Christians have been lowered into the dungeon through a little trap door. They know they will never come out except to die in the arena if they do not die in the dungeon first. Asch describes the scene as one of darkness and horror.

Suddenly the trap door opens and there is a shaft of light as a man is lowered down. As the man descends into this place of darkness, despair, and death he is singing songs of praise and thanksgiving. Word spreads like wildfire through the dungeon, "It's Paul, it's Paul, Paul's here." Paul's joy is so contagious that before long all the people in the dungeon are singing and praising. A whole new spirit has taken over. The emperor has lost; God has won!

The world looks for happiness in circumstances, the believer looks for happiness in God. Why are the persecuted happy? For two reasons. First, because they are looking to God for their reward. Second, because persecution is evidence the other side is losing. Persecution means we have gotten to them and now they are reacting to us. The defeated church is never persecuted because it is not bothering anyone.

As we seek to apply what we have learned in this passage, let me leave you with two questions? The first is, am I really happy? To help answer this question let me make two points. One is: sin robs us of happiness. The sad truth is, Satan tells us that sin will make us happy so we pursue it. Let me tell you something you can take to the bank: Satan is not in the happiness business; he is in the misery business. He will give you just enough pleasure to hook you, then he cranks in the misery. And then he keeps you miserable with a big lie: if you give up the sin you will be even more miserable. While Satan is in the misery business Jesus is in the happiness business.

That brings us to our second point: righteousness is the source of happiness. And that leads to our second question: how can I be happy? Again we need to answer with two points. The first is, happiness begins with forgiveness. In David's prayer of confession in Psalm 51, in verse 12, he asks, "Restore to me the joy of your salvation. . . ." We have already seen that sin robs us of happiness and confession and forgiveness restore it. Some of you have lost the joy of your salvation because of sin in your lives. Why not deal with that sin and have your joy restored.

Our second point is: happiness grows with obedience. You see God loves us and his commands are for our blessing. God is not out to limit us or restrict us. Just the opposite, his commands are given to guide us and protect so we can become all God created us to be. God wants us to be happy, to have real joy. And that is found in a relationship with him and following his ways.

3

Salt and Light

Matthew 5:13–16

Aᴡʜɪʟᴇ ʙᴀᴄᴋ I read about a student from a Christian college who got a summer job in a logging camp. This particular logging camp had a reputation for housing a rough and rowdy crowd. When a friend learned the college student would be working at that camp, the friend told him, "If those lumberjacks find out you're a Christian you're going to be in for a hard time."

The summer passed quickly and the Christian college student returned to school in the fall. His friend asked him how the summer went and if they had given him a hard time for being a Christian. "Oh no," replied the college student, "they didn't give me a bit of trouble. No one ever found out I was a Christian."

The fact is, Jesus Christ wants everyone to find out that we are Christians, that we are Christ followers. As we continue our study in the Sermon on the Mount and continue to learn how to climb with Jesus we will discover that Jesus wants us to be the salt of the earth and the light of the world. The Greek word for *earth* refers to the habitation of humans. The Greek word for *world* refers to humankind, to all people. As Christ-followers we are to affect everyone. In this passage Jesus uses two very common and familiar items to illustrate the influence we are to have in the world.

The first illustration Jesus uses is salt. As in our day, salt was used to flavor food. But in Jesus' day salt had two even more important functions. In fact, salt was so valuable that Roman soldiers in the field were often paid in salt. They could trade it for goods or the local currency. It is from this practice we get the expression, "He's worth his salt."

Salt was a valuable commodity in that day because of two critical functions it performed. The first function of salt was as a preservative. Obviously there was not any refrigeration in ancient Palestine. The Mediterranean world was largely tropical. In that climate foodstuffs, and particularly meat, would go bad and rot very quickly. Salt was the most common preservative and widely used. In the same way, we, as Christians, are to have a preserving effect in the world.

In our day there are two opposing errors related to the Christian's responsibility to the world. The first error is that the world is basically good and with our help it can get better. This view is usually found in liberal circles and it leads to a social gospel. It says humankind can pull itself up by its own bootstraps.

The second error is that the world is getting worse and worse and we as believers should not get involved, rather we should avoid the world, separate ourselves from it, and wait for Christ's return. This view is found in some fundamentalist circles and leads to hyper-separatism. The danger with this view is that it is partially correct. The Bible does teach that the world will get worse and worse resulting in the tribulation and Christ's return. However the Bible does not teach that we are to sit back and watch the world go down the tubes.

It is also true that meat rots and eventually decays. But we can salt meat and delay the decaying process. In the same way, we, as Christ-followers, are to be the salt of the earth. We are to retard the effects of sin in the world. Why are we to retard sin in the world? To provide an opportunity for people to respond to the gospel.

And that brings us to the second function of salt that made it so valuable in those days. Salt creates thirst. We need to remember that Palestine was hot with much open, semi-desert land. The Jews were a pastoral people, herdsmen. The herds and flocks had to be well-watered before they could be moved from one grazing area to another since they often had to cross miles of open, dry land. After cattle and flocks had been at a watering hole for a few days they would not drink deeply because they knew water was readily available. In order to get the animals to drink deeply before moving across a long, hot stretch of land, the herdsmen would put out salt blocks. The salt would make the animals thirsty and they would drink deeply.

Our job is to make men and women thirsty for God. You see, most people are not thirsty for God. Most people do not feel a need for God unless they are facing a crisis. Many of the people you and I know are self-satisfied. How do we make people thirsty for God? By our lives, by our good works as Jesus says in verse 16.

Some years ago my wife, Sandy, and I attended a Gideon's dinner for pastors and their wives. The speaker was a golf pro who had played on the PGA circuit for several years. This man shared how he had no use for God. He believed God was a creation of culture to teach children ethics and comfort the dying. He did not need God.

But on the PGA tour was a group of golfers and their wives who were different from the others. These folks took this golf pro and his wife under their wings. He soon discovered they were Christians. He also found he could argue against their beliefs but he could not argue against their love. Those believers on the PGA tour created a thirst in him and he came to God.

We need to be about the business of laying out salt blocks. In verse 13 Jesus talks about salt becoming tasteless and losing its saltiness. Technically speaking salt cannot lose its saltiness. Sodium chloride is a very stable chemical compound. However, what was commonly called salt in Jesus' day was a white powder obtained from the Dead Sea. The white powder contained sodium chloride along with several other minerals. There were no refineries in those days.

When sodium chloride gets wet it dissolves. When this white powder, called salt, got wet the sodium chloride dissolved but the other minerals remained. The salty taste was gone and the remaining minerals were not good for anything. Each of us needs to examine our lives to see if we have lost our saltiness. The test of whether salt is salty is whether or not it creates thirst for water. The test of whether or not our lives are salty is whether or not we create a thirst for God in others.

When people develop a thirst for God they must be shown the way to God. That brings us to Jesus' second illustration, light. The first function of light is to expose things. The Bible tells us in 2 Corinthians 4:6, "For God who said, 'Let light shine out of the darkness,' is the One who has shone in our hearts to give the light of the knowledge of the glory of God in the face of Christ."

In both the first and eighth chapters of John's gospel account we are told that Jesus is the light of the world. However, here in the Sermon on the Mount, Jesus tells us that we are to be the light of the world. But our light is a reflected light. Jesus is the true light of the world and we reflect his light. It is like the relationship between the sun and the moon. The sun is the true source of light, the moon only reflects sunlight.

Now the moon can be quite bright. On a clear night when there is a full moon in winter and the ground is covered with snow, it can be almost as light as daytime as the moonlight reflects off the snow. However there are times when the earth blocks the light of the sun from the moon and the moon is dark. This is known as a lunar eclipse. Now in the same way the world can come between us and Jesus and his light in our lives is eclipsed. When we allow worldly practices and lifestyles to come into our lives the light of Jesus is eclipsed in our lives.

By the way, while worldliness can include sin, it involves more than sin. When we become consumed with materialism, or careers, or anything else of this world, Jesus' light is eclipsed in our lives. Now please hear me on this. There is nothing wrong with things and there is nothing wrong with having a career and working hard, but when these things have first place in our lives they eclipse the light of Jesus. However, when we brightly reflect the light of Jesus by our good works it exposes people to Jesus.

On a street corner a young boy was holding a mirror in his hand reflecting the light of the sun toward a house. He was centering the reflected light on a second floor window. A man passing by asked the boy what he was doing. The boy explained that his brother was in the house with a prolonged illness and was not able to get outside. The boy said, "Since the sun never enters his room, I'm trying to reflect a little of it in there with this mirror."

As believers that is our job, to reflect Son light into people's lives. Verse 16 says that our good works are to lead people to glorify God. Some people have interpreted this verse to mean that we do not have to say anything about being Christians. We can just let our good works do the talking. But that is not true. Good works without a verbal testimony actually robs God of his glory.

Suppose I decided I could have a greater impact for Christ by working in the secular world. So I resign my pastorate and take a job with a secular company. I further decide to be a witness by my good works. So day after day I am a good and conscientious worker. And week after week I am kind, considerate, and helpful to everyone. I am always cheerful and look for every opportunity to encourage others. Who will get the glory?

Why should anyone give the glory to God? How would they know God had anything to do with it? Why would not people just think I am a great guy and praise me?

Unless we have a verbal testimony to go with our good works, no one will glorify God. We need to share that God is the source of our good works, that we are only reflecting him. In our opening story about the Christian college student and the logging camp, the student behaved properly, he did not compromise his lifestyle, but he was silent so no one found out he was a believer.

Now light does more than expose, it also has a second function, it guides. A businessman from New York City was driving up to Boston. He was ahead of schedule so he decided to get off the interstate and travel some of the back roads so he could enjoy the beautiful New England scenery. After a while he realized he was lost so he stopped in front of an old farm house. A New England farmer sat on the porch and continued to gently rock in his big old rocker. The businessman asked if the farmer knew the way to Interstate 95. "Nope" replied the farmer.

Then the businessman asked if he knew the way to US Highway 1. "Nope," replied the farmer. Finally the businessman asked if he knew the way to the Boston Post Road. Again the farmer replied, "Nope."

Totally exasperated the businessman said, "You don't know how to get anywhere do you?" "Nope," replied the farmer, "But I ain't lost either."

Unfortunately there are a lot of people out on the highways and by-ways of life that are hopelessly lost. The worst part is many of them do not even realize they are lost. We need to show them both their need and the way. We have to be their light to expose them to God and guide them to God.

During the Second World War medical personnel used a system called triage. When there had been a battle and a number of wounded were brought to a field hospital one doctor would give each soldier a quick examination. Then he would place one of three colored tags on the wounded soldier. One tag indicated the soldier's wounds were not severe or life threatening and he could wait to be treated. Another color indicated the soldier was so severely wounded he would probably die anyway. These soldiers were not treated. The third color tag indicated that the soldier was severely wounded but with immediate treatment he would probably survive. These were the soldiers that were rushed into surgery.

Lou had been badly wounded in a major battle and was one of several soldiers brought to a field hospital. The triage doctor briefly looked at Lou and placed a tag on him indicating his case was hopeless and he should not be treated. However a nurse noticed that Lou was conscious and began to talk to him. They discovered they were both from Ohio. Getting to know Lou, she could not just let him die. Breaking all the rules she changed his tag. He was rushed into surgery. After months in the hospital Lou recovered. He met another nurse in the hospital who later became his wife. He went on to live a full and happy life all because a nurse changed his tag.

And that is our job as believers, to go around changing people's tags. Satan has tagged people for death and damnation. But Jesus has given us the job of changing people's tags. That is what being salt and light is all about. How do we do it? For our application I want to share with you ten ways to change people's tags.

The first is to target one or two people. If we try to reach everyone we will reach no one. However, if we target someone we may reach that one, a friend, a family member, a neighbor, a coworker, someone you can be salt and light to. Second, pray for them every day. Ask God to soften their hearts. Ask God to give you opportunities and the courage to share with them. Third, enlist others to pray with you for them. Get others praying for you to be able to change their tags. Fourth, contact them once a week. A card, a note, an email, a call, in some way reach out to them each week.

Fifth, spend time with them once a month. Play golf, go bowling, have them over for a meal or go out for a meal, go to a show, a game, find some activity you can share with them. Build a common bond. Sixth, invite them to a church activity once a quarter. Do not necessarily invite them to a church service, but to a women's outing, a men's breakfast, a potluck, or something nonthreatening. Seventh, invite them to a church service every six months. Invite them to Christmas or Easter services or some other special service. By the way the best way to invite someone to church is to also invite them out to eat or over to eat before or after the service.

Eighth, share Christ with them when the opportunity presents itself. Do not force it, wait for God's timing. Do not preach at them; share what God is doing in your life. Put out salt blocks and shed some light. Ninth, introduce them to Christian friends. Pick people with winsome personalities and strong testimonies. Have them over with Christian friends for desert or games or some other social event. Create opportunities for them to be with contagious Christians.

Tenth, expect them to respond to the gospel. People take their cue from us and our nonverbal behavior and attitudes. If we do not expect them to respond we will communicate that in our actions and attitudes and they probably will not respond. But, if we expect them to respond, there is every chance they will. After all God is on our side and he has told us to be salt and light. God's plan was to use us to draw people to himself, let us be salt and light.

4

Beyond the Law

Matthew 5:17–26

THE MAN WHO MAY have had a greater impact on American education than any other person is the Swiss psychologist Jean Piaget. Piaget's writings and theories began to impact American education in the late 50's and early 60's. Roger Brown, former Professor of Psychology at Harvard University, has said: "After Freud, it is Jean Piaget who has made the greatest contribution to modern psychology." While others with psychological training might dispute this ranking, no one with any knowledge of psychology would deny the tremendous contributions of Jean Piaget.

Like Freud, Piaget was interested in human development. However his approach to the study of human development differed sharply. Whereas Freud studied his patients, neurotic and psychotic adults, probing their memories to study their childhood experiences, Piaget studied normal children and adults to discover the stages children pass through on their way to adulthood.

A basic premise of Piaget's theory is that children are not miniature adults. They do not think like adults only on a simpler level. Their thinking processes are different. Piaget outlines a series of stages children pass through from child-like thinking to adult-like thinking. Piaget's research strategy involved careful observation and some clever experiments.

One experiment involved distinguishing between different perceptions of naughtiness. Piaget discovered that children between three to six years of age perceived naughtiness in terms of behavior rather than intention while children over six years of age were able to take intentions into account. To demonstrate the phenomena, Piaget told two stories to children in both age groups.

The first story involved a boy who was called to come to supper. He obediently came right away. But as he did he accidentally bumped into the table and five dishes fell to the floor and broke. The second story was about a boy who was told not to take any cookies from the kitchen counter. When his mother left the room he reached up on the counter to take a cookie and knocked over one dish and it broke.

After hearing the stories the children were asked which boy deserved the greater punishment. As adults we would obviously say the second boy because, while he broke only one dish, he broke it during an act of disobedience. The first child may have broken more dishes but he did so accidentally while obeying.

However, remember, Piaget found that children think differently than adults. What he found was that children under six years of age thought the first boy should get the greater punishment because he broke more dishes. Young children cannot take intention into account.

The Bible tells us in 1 Corinthians 14:20 that we should not be children in our thinking. God had given his law to his people in the Old Testament. By Jesus' day the Pharisees had codified the law into 615 rules. For example, they had dozens of rules for how to keep the Sabbath. However their legalistic system was based strictly on outward behavior. It had no concern for the attitudes and intentions that lay behind the behavior.

The approach of the Pharisees to the law was like that of young children. They were only concerned with outward behavior not intentions and motives. In Matthew 5:17–26 we discover how Jesus' understanding of the law differed from the Pharisees. We see how Jesus takes us beyond the letter of the law to the spirit of the law.

The Pharisees often accused Jesus of doing away with the law. In verses 17–19 Jesus says nothing could be further from the truth. He declares, "Do you think I have come to abolish the law or the prophets? I have come not to abolish . . . them." What is Jesus referring to when he speaks of the law and the prophets?

The word *law* had two meanings. In its narrowest sense it referred to the 10 commandments. In a broader sense it referred to the five books of Moses, the Torah. In this verse Jesus is using a common phrase, "the law and the prophets." In this context the law referred to the five books of Moses: Genesis, Exodus, Leviticus, Numbers, and Deuteronomy. The prophets referred to the rest of the Old Testament.

What Jesus was saying, in essence, was, I have not come to abolish the teachings of the Old Testament. Then what had he come to do? He tells us in verse 17, "I have come to fulfill them." The word *fulfill* has the sense of completing. Christ had come to complete the law. How did Christ come to fulfill or complete the law? He fulfilled the law by becoming subject to the law and going to the cross to satisfy the demands of the law. He died, not for his violations of the law, but for ours. Jesus Christ's death frees us from the power of the law and the indwelling of the Holy Spirit empowers us to live up to the spirit of the law. We will come back to this point, but right now let us return to Jesus' view of the law.

In verse 18 Jesus says the law represents God's moral standards for this world, none of its demands for holiness will be modified as long as heaven and earth exist. Then in verse 19 Jesus talks about keeping and teaching the law. He says anyone who puts aside any of the demands of the law, regardless of how insignificant the person thinks it is, and teaches others to do the same, will be the least in the kingdom of heaven. On the other hand, the one who keeps and teaches the law will be great in the kingdom.

There are two points in verse 19 we should note. The first is, there is a gradation of rewards in eternity. This truth is taught in the parable of the talents. It is also taught in 1 Corinthians 3:12–15, where we read: "If anyone builds on this foundation using, gold, silver, costly stones, wood, hay or straw, their work will be shown for what it is, because the Day will bring it to light. It will be revealed with fire, and the fire will test the quality of each person's work. If what they have built survives they will receive their reward. If it is burned up they will suffer loss, they themselves will be saved, but only as one escaping through the flames."

Now, some of you may be thinking, our motivation for obeying and serving God should be love not rewards. Yes, you are right, it should be. The Bible tells us in the book of Revelation that our rewards will be used as love gifts to give to God.

The second point is, we teach by our behavior. That is, we teach by example. We find a negative illustration of this type of teaching by example in the second chapter of Galatians. In verses 11–13, we read, "When Peter came to Antioch, I opposed him to his face, because he was clearly in the wrong. Before certain men came from James, he used to eat with the gentiles. But when they arrived, he began to draw back and separate himself from the gentiles because he was afraid of those who belonged to the circumcision group. The other Jews joined him in his hypocrisy, so that by their hypocrisy even Barnabas was led astray." Even as other believers were watching Peter and were led astray by his example, so others are watching us.

Now, you may say, other believers should not be watching me, they should have their eyes on Jesus. That sounds pious and good, but, the fact is, other believers are watching us. Especially younger and weaker believers. The Bible clearly teaches in 1 Thessalonians 1:7, Titus 2:7, and many other places that we are to set a positive example for other believers. In our American culture with its strong emphasis on individualism and self-reliance, we sometimes forget that we are our brothers' and sisters' keepers. We need to remember that others are watching us and our actions will either lead them astray or lead them the right way.

Then, in verse 20, Jesus moves beyond the law with a very provocative statement, he says, "For I tell you that unless your righteousness surpasses that of the Pharisees and the teachers of the law, you will certainly not enter the kingdom of heaven." Jesus makes two points in this verse.

The first point is, the righteousness of the scribes and Pharisees is not good enough to get to heaven. God called his people to be a holy people and had given them the law to show them the way. The Pharisees had built up a tradition around the law and lived by that tradition rather than the law. As we have already seen they had 615 rules in their tradition.

The Pharisees taught that if you kept all the rules you could get to heaven. However their rules were only concerned with external actions. The Pharisees had interpreted the law of God to only apply to outward behavior. They were not concerned with the inner attitudes and intentions that lead to the acts. They were concerned with murder but not the hate or vengeance that led to murder. They were concerned with adultery but not the lust that led to it. They were concerned with stealing but not the greed, materialism, and jealousy that led to it. That approach falls short of the holiness of God.

We find an example of how the tradition of the Pharisees violated the spirit of the law in Mark's gospel account. In chapter 7, verses 9 to 13, we read Jesus' words to the Pharisees: "You have a fine way of setting aside the commands of God in order to observe your own traditions! For Moses said, 'Honor your father and mother,' and 'Anyone who curses his father or mother must be put to death.' But you say that if a man says to his father or mother: 'Whatever help you might otherwise have received from me is Corban (that is a gift devoted to God), then you no longer let him do anything for his father or mother. Thus you nullify the Word of God by your tradition. . . ."

The Pharisees came up with a rule that you could dedicate your money to the temple and this money could no longer be used to help your parents. Now, here was the catch. While the money was dedicated to the temple it did not necessarily have to go to the temple. You could spend this money on yourself, just not others.

This leads to the second point Jesus makes in verse 20. We are to be more righteous than the scribes and Pharisees to get to heaven. Now, you may ask, how do we do that? These were some pretty righteous dudes. Did they keep 98 percent of the rules and we have to keep 99 percent? No! Jesus is not talking about quantity of righteousness but quality of righteousness. No human can ever be righteous enough to make it to heaven. You and I cannot be good enough. But everyone can receive God's righteousness by faith in Jesus Christ.

And that leads to two more points. First, the righteousness of the scribes and Pharisees was legalism, which looks at behavior. Second, the righteousness of Jesus is holiness, which looks at the heart attitude. It is a right attitude that leads to right behavior. In the verses that follow Jesus says over and over again, "You have heard it said . . . but I tell you." When Jesus says, "You have heard it said . . ." he is referring to the Pharisees legalistic interpretation of the law. And when Jesus says, "I tell you . . ." he is moving beyond the letter of the law to the spirit of the law.

In this chapter we will look at one example of this in verses 21–26 and then look at Jesus other examples in the next two chapters. Jesus begins with the straightforward command of the law, "Do not murder." And then he adds the saying from the tradition of the Pharisees, "anyone who murders will be subject to judgment." The Pharisees were only concerned with outward behavior and its consequences. But Jesus was concerned with the heart attitude. It is the heart attitude that leads to murder.

Let me ask you a question: If you could push a button and eliminate another person with no consequences to yourself, would you do it? Several years ago this question was posed to the readers of *Psychology Today* magazine. Sixty percent of the respondents said they would push the button. They were also asked who they would push the button on. The respondents replied current spouses, ex-mates, bosses, neighbors, criminals, and politicians. One respondent posed an intriguing question, "If such a device were available, would anyone be alive to tell about it?

Sometimes the only difference between someone who murders and someone who does not is fear and opportunity. What Jesus is saying is that the act results from the inner person, from the attitude, from the heart. Jesus says our attitude is as important as our behavior. The way to deal with murder is not to concentrate on the behavior but the heart.

In verse 22 Jesus says that in God's eyes attacking a person verbally is just as serious as attacking them physically. How can that be? Because both verbal assault and physical assault come from the same motives, anger and hate.

Jesus takes us beyond the letter of the law to the spirit of the law and tells us how to deal with anger and hate. His solution is straightforward. In verses 23–26 Jesus says go to the other person and straighten things out. If you are at fault apologize, seek forgiveness and make restitution. If the other is at fault offer reconciliation and forgiveness.

In the comic section of many Sunday newspapers is a comic strip called "Sally Forth." Let me share with you a strip that appeared in the paper a few years ago. Sally is in the kitchen pouting and her husband Ted is in the living room pouting. Sally is thinking, "Why is it that our fights are usually over dumb, little things?"

Then she thinks, "It was silly of us to have that argument. I suppose I better make the first move to patch things up." So Sally goes into the living room and sits by her husband, Ted. She says, "One thing that helps a relationship work is a willingness to resolve conflict." Then she adds, "I want you to know that I'm willing to accept your apology." With that Ted turns and looks at her with a scowl. In the final frame Sally puts her arm around Ted and says, "Just a little levity to break the ice."

Sally had the right idea. Regardless of who is at fault or who started it, we should be the first to seek to resolve it. Now, I can hear some of you saying, "But he always starts it," or "I'm always the one to give in," or "she needs to make the first move." Jesus said, "Blessed are the peacemakers." To look at who started it or who always makes the first move is legalism. True spirituality moves to resolve it. To those of you who always seem to end up making the first move, I say, "Great! Keep it up!"

As we seek to apply what we have studied I would like to leave you with three thoughts. The first thought is: You cannot make it to heaven by keeping the law. Many of the scribes and Pharisees lived very upright and moral lives. They kept all the religious rules and regulations to the extent it was humanly possible. Yet Jesus said it was not good enough.

The Bible tells us in James 2:10, "Whoever keeps the whole law and yet stumbles in one point has become guilty of all." Let me illustrate this truth. Suppose you were hanging from a cliff by a chain with ten links. Would it matter if one link broke? Two? All ten? Of course not, whether one link broke or all ten, the result would be the same. You would plunge to your death. So it is with God's moral law, whether we have violated one or a dozen commandments the result is the same. Our sin has separated us from God.

There are only two ways to get to heaven. One is by being perfect, by never, ever committing a single sin. If you tell me you have never sinned, then I know at least one of your sins, lying. Since that route of perfection leaves all of us out we need to look at the second way to get to heaven. It is by faith in Jesus Christ and his death for our sin. Jesus said in John 14:6, "I am the Way, the Truth, and the Life. No one comes to the father but through me." The Apostle Peter said in Acts 4:12, "There is no other name under heaven given to us by which we must be saved." And the Apostle Paul, in 1 Timothy 2:5–6 said, "There is one God and one mediator between God and us, Christ Jesus, who gave his life as a ransom for all."

If you have been trusting in good works or religion to get you to heaven, then if you are not more righteous and more religious than the Pharisees, you do not have a chance. But if you come to God, admit you have sinned, and ask him to forgive you because Jesus died for your sins, he will come to live with you in your life through the Holy Spirit, and when you die he will take you to spend forever with him. You can reach out to God right where you are.

The second thought I want to leave with you is: You cannot live a fulfilled Christian life by legalism. If your life is run by a set of rules, by lists of "do's and don'ts," allow the Holy Spirit to set you free from rules so you can life by the spirit of the law, led and controlled by the Spirit. Rules are external controls. The fulfilled Christian life is lived by the internal control of the Holy Spirit.

The final thought I want to leave you with is: You can live beyond the law by being a peacemaker. When conflict comes up at home, on the job, at school, even at church, be the first to seek reconciliation. Maybe there is someone you need to contact as soon as possible to make things right. As

Jesus points out in verses 23 and 24, when there is something between us and another person, there is something between us and God.

We can live beyond the letter of the law in the freedom of the spirit of the law through the power of the Holy Spirit. Remember, God's laws were given to guide us and protect us and help us become all he created us to be. God loves you! God is on your side! God wants the best for you! Give him a chance!

5

Beyond the Law—Part II

Matthew 5:27–32

WHILE I WAS A student at Wheaton Graduate School, I had a job working for a chain of discount stores called Turnstyle. They were similar to a Target or a Walmart. I was assistant to the manager of the hardware department. This chain of stores, as most stores do, had a significant problem with shoplifting. In fact they estimated that 10 percent of the price of every item went to cover theft. Each store had its own security personnel.

In addition all managers and clerks were trained to spot and deter shoplifting. There were certain behaviors we were trained to look for. If we saw someone exhibiting those behaviors we were to go to that person and ask if we could help them. Then we were to busy ourselves straightening merchandise in the aisle by the person. I am sure there were people who intended to shoplift something but were prevented by the presence of store personnel.

Turnstyle had a policy of having all shoplifters arrested. But they could not have a person arrested for intending to shoplift. Only those who actually engaged in shoplifting could be arrested. American criminal law is not concerned with what a person is thinking about doing or intends to do. The law is only concerned with what a person actually does.

However God's law is concerned with what a person thinks of doing. God is just as concerned with what a person thinks of doing as with what the person actually does. As we saw in the last chapter, the scribes and Pharisees of Jesus' day had developed a tradition and long list of rules around God's law. That tradition was only concerned with outward actions and totally ignored inner attitudes. In Matthew 5:27–32 we find Jesus continuing to contrast the Pharisees' tradition and the spirit of the law. Here Jesus tackles the issue of sexual immorality and takes us beyond the letter of the law to the spirit of the law.

First Jesus looks at immoral thoughts. In verse 27 Jesus quotes the seventh commandment. He says, "You have heard it said, 'Do not commit adultery.'" This command was concerned with the act of adultery. With their emphasis on outward behavior, the Pharisees ignored the tenth commandment, which said a man should not covet his neighbor's wife. In their view the Pharisees had kept the law if they did not commit the act. With this approach they had conveniently narrowed the definition of sexual sin and broadened the definition of sexual purity. In verse 28 Jesus takes us beyond the letter of the law to the spirit of the law when he says, "But I tell you that anyone who looks at a woman lustfully has already committed adultery with her in his heart."

Before we go any further there are two points we need to make to understand this passage. The first is, there is not the slightest suggestion in this passage, or for that matter anywhere in the Bible, that sexual desire or sexual intimacy within the commitment of marriage are anything but God-given and beautiful.

The Old and New Testaments stand alone among the holy books of the major religions of the world in their view of the human body and the sanctification of sex in marriage. It was God who created us male and female. It was God who created our sex drives. Our sexuality is not part of our fallen nature, it is part of God's original creation and he declared it good. Nowhere in the Bible is sex ever seen as evil. It is only the misuse of sex that is wrong. You see, while it is true that God created us as sexual beings and gave us our sex drives, it is also true that God has given us guidelines within which to exercise our sexuality.

Physical Intimacy has two functions. One function is for reproduction. The second function is the bonding together of a man and woman in marriage. Sex is God's gift of love and life. Our sexuality was meant to find its expression in marriage and any other expression of it is sin.

Now some may want to see God as a narrow-minded killjoy. They may see God's guidelines as restrictive and limiting. But they are wrong. God's commands were not given to restrict us. Just the opposite, they were given to free us to become all we could be. God designed us and created us and he knows what is best for us.

A couple of years ago, for my birthday, my children all chipped in and bought me a laptop computer. Now the laptop came with an instruction manual. The instruction manual was written by the manufacturer of the computer. When I received the computer I had a choice. I could read and follow the manual or ignore it. The manual was written to help me get the most out of my computer. I was free to ignore the manual but the result would have been that I would not have gotten the full benefit of the computer. In fact I might damage the computer and lose all use of it.

So it is with God's Word, the owner's manual for the human race, we ignore it at our own peril. The Bible tells us in Galatians 6:7–8, "Do not be deceived: God cannot be mocked. People reap what they sow. The one who sows to please the sinful nature, from that nature will reap destruction. . . ."

We can see the results of violating God's commands all around us. One out of three babies in our country is conceived out of wedlock. Half of all firstborns were conceived out of wedlock. Two out of three babies born in our nation's capital are conceived out of wedlock. Unmarried women have over a million abortions each year. Sexually transmitted diseases are the number one communicable diseases in America. Half of all high school students will contract a sexually transmitted disease before they graduate. More Americans will get a sexually transmitted disease than the flu this year. Thousands of Americans will die from AIDS. Thousands of others will lose sexual functions or reproductive capacity as a result of sexually transmitted diseases. God's commands are not designed to restrict us. Rather they are designed to protect us and free us to fully enjoy our sexuality as God intended.

The second point we need to understand is, while Jesus refers specifically to men lusting after women, what he taught applies to both men and women. The context here, as we learned in the first chapter, is Jesus is addressing his disciples, who were men, and not a mixed audience. Jesus is using one case to illustrate a broader point. Lust by a man or woman, married or single, is immoral, it is equivalent to committing the act. Jesus recognized that the real source of sexual sin is the thought life.

In verses 29–30 he tells us how to deal with this, "If your right eye causes you to sin, gouge it out and throw it away. It is better for you to lose one part of your body than for your whole body to be thrown into hell. And if your right hand causes you to sin, cut it off and throw it away. It is better for you to lose one part of your body than for your whole body to go into hell."

Jesus is not talking about literally mutilating ourselves; he is using a dramatic figure of speech. What Jesus is saying is that we must be ruthless in rooting immorality out of our lives. We must be ready to take the most drastic action necessary. For example, for some it may mean getting rid of cable TV, for others it may mean a filter on our computer and the computer in a public place, for others it may mean avoiding the video store. Jesus is saying, do whatever it takes.

We live in a sex-saturated society. The types of movies that used to be shown in seedy theaters in the wrong part of town are now piped into our living rooms by cable or satellite. Movies we would never go to the theater to watch come into our homes as video rentals. When I was a teenager they would not show Elvis Presley on TV because they thought the way he swung his hips was obscene. Today you can see music videos on MTV that make Elvis look like a prude.

Many soap operas, both daytime and primetime, are pornographic in their content. We see so many people hopping into and out of bed so frequently on TV that we have come to accept it as normal. We see no problem with people being depicted as sleeping together outside of marriage unless it shows them nude.

A few years ago there was a made-for-TV movie called "Choices." It was about a man whose teenage daughter was pregnant. He thought it was wrong for her to have an abortion. In trying to talk his daughter out of an abortion he says to her, "Haven't I taught you any morals?" The irony was that the father was concerned about his daughter having an abortion, but he was not concerned about his unmarried daughter having sex. Our culture totally twists morality. We need to take drastic action to deal with the immorality we are subjected to.

Let me suggest three specific actions we can take. First we need to accept our sexuality. We need to recognize that God created us as sexual beings and gave us our sex drives. Now our sex drive can be misused just like our hunger drive. Without our hunger drive we'd starve to death. But if we abuse it we practice gluttony. In the same way we can misuse our sex drive.

And that leads to the second action: we need to confess our sexual sins to God. Many of us may never engage in immoral acts but what about our thought lives. Do we think about things we would never actually do? Jesus said the thoughts were as bad as the actions. We need to confess our impure thoughts and ask God to cleanse our minds. Whether we have sinned in thought or action we need to confess our sin to God and seek his forgiveness.

The third action is: we need to avoid sources of temptation. The Bible tells us in 1 Corinthians 10:13 that God will make a way for us to escape any temptation. And the Bible tells us in 2 Timothy 2:22 that we should flee evil desires. Now we cannot actually flee our evil desires, but we can flee the sources of those desires. We may need to change our reading habits or TV watching habits. We may need to avoid certain forms of entertainment. No matter how radical the changes need to be, Jesus says we need to make them.

By the way, the rest of 2 Timothy 2:22 says, ". . . and pursue righteousness, faith, love and peace along with those who call on the Lord out of a pure heart." The fact is, pornography and other sources of lust can be as addictive as any drug. It is often very difficult to flee these things on our own. Often we need help and support and that is what the church is all about. We were not meant to do it alone. We need to talk to our pastor or find a Christian support group.

In verses 31 and 32 Jesus moves from immoral thoughts to immoral actions when he says, "It has been said, 'Anyone who divorces his wife must give her a certificate of divorce.' But I tell you that anyone who divorces his wife, except for marital unfaithfulness, causes her to become an adulteress, and anyone who marries the divorced woman commits adultery."

Now, I recognize that divorce is a sensitive subject. Some of you reading this have been touched by it. Some of you have deep scars and some of you are still experiencing pain. Some of you may be right in the middle of a divorce. The Bible deals with reality, it touches the most intimate areas of our lives.

These verses here in chapter 5 are a summary of Jesus teaching on divorce. We find a fuller account in Matthew 19:3–9, where we read, "Some Pharisees came to [Jesus] to test him. They asked, 'Is it lawful for a man to divorce his wife for every and any reason?' 'Haven't you read,' he replied, 'that the creator made them male and female, and said, "For this reason a man will leave his father and mother and be united to his wife, and the two will become one flesh." So they are no longer two, but one. Therefore what God has joined together, let man not separate.' 'Why then,' they asked, 'did Moses command that a man give his wife a certificate of divorce and send her away?' Jesus replied, 'Moses permitted you to divorce your wives because your hearts were hard. But it was not this way from the beginning. I tell you that anyone who divorces his wife, except for marital unfaithfulness, and marries another woman commits adultery.'"

To understand this passage we need to look at the cultural background. Jesus is responding to a question from the Pharisees. They had a debate over what Moses meant in Deuteronomy 24:1 when he wrote, "If a man marries a woman who becomes displeasing to him because he finds something indecent about her, and he writes her a certificate of divorce, gives it to her and sends her from his house. . . ."

The Pharisees brought their debate to Jesus. There were two schools of thought about what Moses meant by "something indecent." The conservative school of Shammi argued it referred to sexual immorality. The liberal school of Hillel argued it referred to anything that displeased the husband. The Pharisees who questioned Jesus seemed to have been from the liberal school of Hillel since they asked, "Is it lawful for a man to divorce his wife for any and every reason?"

Jesus' answer to the Pharisees was in three parts. We will look at each part separately because in each part he takes issue with the Pharisees and goes beyond the letter of the law to the spirit of the law. First, the Pharisees were concerned with the grounds for divorce while Jesus was interested in the basis for marriage. The Pharisees turned to the Law of Moses for their question, Jesus turned to the creation account for his answer. What Jesus was saying, in essence, is, "Let's see what God's original intention was." He points out that God's original intention was for marriage to be a lifetime commitment between a man and a woman.

Second, the Pharisees called Moses' teaching a command, Jesus called it a concession to the hardness of their hearts. Jesus points out that this was not God's plan, he says, "But it was not this way from the beginning. . . ." God's original plan was for a lifetime commitment, divorce for unfaithfulness was a concession to human sinfulness.

Third, the Pharisees saw divorce as a privilege, Jesus saw it as a breakdown of God's plan and a serious matter. In fact, Jesus saw divorce as so serious, that, with one exception, he called remarriage after divorce adultery. The exception was marital unfaithfulness.

This exception clause has been the source of some controversy in Evangelical circles. Sincere, Bible-believing Christians have differing views on how to understand and apply this teaching. I will share my understanding. I do not believe an act of adultery is grounds for divorce rather it is grounds for forgiveness. If a person commits adultery and then confesses to their mate and asks forgiveness, the clear teaching of Scripture is to forgive. We have a classic example of this in the Old Testament book of Hosea where his wife committed adultery and he forgave her and took her back.

However when a husband or wife leaves his or her mate and lives with another person this is an act of continuous adultery which ends the marriage. This is the understanding of Bible teachers such as John MacArthur and Chuck Swindoll and I see it the same way. I also recognize other sincere believers do not agree with this understanding. I respect their right to their views and understand their need to be faithful to their understanding of the Bible. However the one thing we can all agree on is that God intended marriage to be a lifetime commitment. And we can all work to heal hurting marriages.

We have dealt with some very touchy and controversial subjects in this chapter. How do we apply Jesus' teaching in our lives? Let me leave you with two thoughts by way of application. First, we need to get beyond the letter of the law to the spirit of the law when it comes to sexual immorality. It is not enough to deal with behavior, we also have to deal with our thought lives. Some of us are watching things we should not be watching, visiting websites we should not be visiting, and reading things we should not be reading.

We need to be careful what we put in our minds. We may think our thought life is private and does not affect anyone else. But that is not true. When a person watches pornography it will affect their marriage. The Bible tells us in Philippians 4:8, "Whatever is true, whatever is pure, whatever is lovely, whatever is admirable, if anything is excellent or praiseworthy, think about such things."

Then there may be some of you reading this who may be dealing with the pain of divorce. What should the attitude of the church be toward those who have experienced divorce? It should be one of love, understanding and acceptance. Not necessarily acceptance of the divorce, but acceptance of the person. All of us have blown it, if not in this area, then in some other area. None of us is in a position to judge each other but all of us should be in a position to minister to each other. We need to move beyond the letter of the law to the spirit of the law and show grace and love.

To those of you who have experienced divorce God loves you and cares about you. He wants to meet you where you are and work with you.

And there are some of you that have been divorced against. You did not want the divorce; you wanted to try to work things out, but your former mate left. No matter how you find yourself divorced I want you to know that God loves you and there is place for you in the church. If you are still dealing with the impact of divorce find a Christian support group or talk with your pastor.

The second thought is: staying legally married while being emotionally divorced is hypocrisy and legalism. Yes, you still live together. You present yourself in public as husband and wife but in the home you are merely roommates tolerating each other. That is legalism. You may be living up to the letter of the law but you are not following the spirit of the law.

Again these are some difficult issues we are dealing with, and in many instances there are not any quick and simple answers, but there are answers in the Word of God. Also I want you to know that your pastors are there to teach what the Word of God says, not to judge anyone. Just the opposite they are there to help and minister to people. If you are struggling in any of these areas we have discussed, I would suggest you find a godly pastor to talk about these issues with you and guide you into God's Word.

I want you to know that I come not as someone who has all the answers and has it all together, I come as fellow struggler and a fellow learner. Together we can go to God's Word and find some answers. It is my prayer that all of us can begin to live beyond the letter of the law and by the spirit of the law. In the Sermon on the Mount Jesus is inviting us to climb with him to higher ground in every area of our lives. By his grace and with each other's help we can do it!

6

Beyond the Law—Part III

Matthew 5:33–48

KEITH MILLER TELLS ABOUT an experience he had as director of a retreat center. He had the idea of having people who had accepted Christ at a retreat come back a couple of months later and share what had happened since they accepted Christ as their Savior. The first person to return to share was an attractive young homemaker with a beautiful family named Ann. Keith had selected her because she had was quite articulate.

Keith was excited when Ann got up to speak. He anticipated that this would be a great experience. The pretty young homemaker came to the front of the room and said, "I'm sorry, I wish I could tell you something exciting has happened in my life since I gave it to Christ but in my case nothing has happened."

Miller says that his worst fears were realized at that moment. Desperately, from where he was sitting he said, "Ann, why don't you just describe the past month for us." Miller wanted her to talk long enough for him to think of a way of saving the situation.

After thinking for a moment, Ann began: "Well, I guess my husband and I were having a pretty rough time when I came here last month. After I committed my life to Christ I decided I was going to spend some time just listening to Ben talk about his business. I hadn't been interested in doing this in the past. So I just started listening to him. And this week we decided to take a trip together, just the two of us, to spend some time together without the kids. We haven't done that in a long time. I guess, maybe you'd say we're getting along better in several ways.

And my kids, you suggested that weekend that we listen to our children. So I started to spend some time with them." Smiling, Ann continued, "I guess we're getting along a little better too. And my mother, I've been visiting her this month, for Jesus' sake, because I couldn't do it for my sake. My mother cried when I came to see her this week."

Pausing for a moment to think Ann added, "Oh, yes, I started inviting my neighbors over for coffee about two week ago. Some of them are pretty lonely and I've tried listen to them." Ann thought for a few more seconds before shaking her head and saying, a little sadly and very seriously, "I'm sorry Keith, but I can't say anything really important has happened in my life since I committed it to Christ."

How much all of us are like Ann. We so easily overlook or take for granted all the little things God is doing in our lives because we are so busy looking for the dramatic and the spectacular. I believe the real test of our faith comes, not so much in the crises of our lives, but in the routine of everyday living. If our faith is real it should it should make a difference in our everyday lives, in our homes, on the job, at school, and at church.

As we continue our study of the Sermon on the Mount we are learning to climb with Jesus. In Matthew 5:33–48 we again find ourselves in the section of the Sermon on the Mount where Jesus challenges the Pharisees' interpretation of the Law. As we have seen the Pharisees had developed a tradition around the law that consisted of hundreds of rules a person was expected to keep. However, the tradition of the Pharisees was a legalistic interpretation of the law that was only concerned with outward behavior.

In this section of the Sermon on the Mount, Jesus has been taking us beyond the letter of the law to the spirit of the law. Jesus has already dealt with murder and hate as well as adultery, lust and divorce. Here in Matthew 5:33–48, Jesus deals with honesty, peace, and love, three characteristics that affect our everyday lives and determine how we deal with the routine of life.

The first characteristic that Jesus deals with is honesty. In verse 33 he says, "Again you have heard that it was said to the people long ago, 'Do not break your oath, but keep the oaths you have made to the Lord.'" These words are a compilation of three Old Testament passages: Leviticus 19:12; Numbers 30:2; and Deuteronomy 23:21. The idea in these verses is, if you make a vow to God, or a vow to someone in God's name, you were obligated to keep it. Making a vow to someone in God's name was equivalent to making a vow to God.

The point behind this commandment was to teach that promises made to others were as sacred as promises made to God. God wanted his people to be honest and trustworthy in all their dealings. The Pharisees had twisted the law so that their tradition taught that a person only had to be honest when they were under oath.

So in verses 34–37 Jesus takes beyond the letter of the law to the spirit of the law. What Jesus is saying in these verses is that we should be honest all the time not just when we are under oath. In fact Jesus says it would be better for us not to use oaths at all if they cause us to be dishonest. Jesus says all we need are *yes* and *no*. Since we are to be honest all the time nothing more is needed. Honesty should permeate our lives.

One of the most honest men I have ever known was my father. Each year, when I had my spring break from school my father would take a week's vacation and we would go fishing in upstate Pennsylvania. My father was a fly fisherman and he loved fly fishing in the mountain rivers and streams. I did not have the patience for fly fishing so I would dig for worms, put them on a hook, and fish. I usually caught more fish than my dad, but he thought I cheated.

The year I was 16 he let me drive the car on some deserted country roads where there was no traffic. I did not have my license yet. It was early spring and there were still icy patches in the shaded parts of the road. I hit an icy patch, lost control of the car, and we ended up in a ditch with considerable damage to the car. The car was drivable so he drove it home and took it to a body shop to be repaired. The repairs came to several hundred dollars, a great deal of money at that time. The accident had occurred on a lonely country road. There were no witnesses and the police did not investigate.

Since I did not have a driver's license my father's insurance would not cover the accident. The manager of the body shop suggested my father file a claim saying he was driving and the insurance would cover it. Now, at that time, our family was going through some financial hard times and I am sure that suggestion was a real temptation for my dad. But without a moment's hesitation, my father told the body shop manager that it would be dishonest and he could not do it. That incident made a tremendous impression on me.

There are times we may be tempted to stretch the truth, but the truth does not stretch, it breaks. There are no such things as white lies and fibs. Either something is true or it is not. We need to let our *yes* be *yes* and our *no* be *no*.

As Christ-followers we should be known as honest and we should also be known as peacemakers. Again Jesus begins with the letter of the law in verse 38 when he says, "You have heard it said, 'Eye for eye and tooth for tooth.'" And, again, the Pharisees had misinterpreted the law. The Pharisees had twisted the law to mean they had the right to take revenge on anyone who harmed them. Their tradition taught it was okay to pay back evil for evil. They let their tradition supersede the law.

This commandment is not referring to personal revenge but to judicial punishment. What it is saying is, let the punishment fit the crime. There is a difference between personal revenge and justice. Revenge is concerned with appeasing our hate and vengefulness, justice is concerned with protecting society. Criminals need to be punished, not so their victims can be avenged, but to protect society. A law God had given to protect society was being used by the Pharisees to justify personal revenge.

And so once again Jesus takes us beyond the letter of the law to the spirit of the law. In verses 39–42 he teaches us to seek peace by giving up our rights. Christ goes on to discuss four specific rights we need to surrender to be peacemakers. First, in verse 39, he teaches we need to surrender the right to retaliation.

Now some students of the Bible have used this verse and Matthew 5:9 where Jesus said, "Blessed are the peacemakers…" to say that he taught pacifism. Personally I have great respect for pacifists. I believe we can learn much from them. And I would defend their right to follow pacifism as a personal philosophy, but I disagree with them in their understanding of what Jesus is teaching. A slap on the cheek in that culture was not considered a physical attack but an insult. Jesus is not discussing resisting a physical attack but not repaying an insult. The teaching here is about not seeking revenge not an argument for pacifism.

Again, I am not arguing against pacifism, I am only saying that this passage does not teach it. Also, even for persons who choose to defend themselves when attacked, there is a difference between self-defense and vengeance. For example, if someone were to falsely accuse me of wrongdoing I may choose to defend myself by denying it. But when I begin making accusations against the other person, even if they are true, I am retaliating. Jesus Christ says that to be peacemakers we must not retaliate.

Then, in verse 40, we find the second right we need to surrender to be peacemakers, the right to our possessions. As long as we view our possessions as our own we become selfish, defensive and greedy. But when we view our possessions as a trust from God, as a stewardship, then we become generous and sharing. We no longer need to become defensive. The Bible tells us in James 4:1–3 that quarrels, fights, and wars come from greed and selfishness. Peace comes from generosity and sharing.

Next, in verse 41 we find the third right we need to surrender to be peacemakers, the right to our time. God gives us every breath we breathe. Our time is a gift and stewardship from God. Time is not ours, it is God's. We are to be stewards of every resource God gives us, including time.

Sandy and I met in a church in New Jersey. The pastor of that church was a giant of a man in more ways than one. He stood six foot, six inches tall and was very dignified. His appearance was sometimes intimidating but he was a kind and caring man. I would often stop by the church to talk with him. In spite of his busy schedule, sermon preparation, and other responsibilities, if he was in, he always had time for me. When I came into his study he acted as though he had nothing better to do than talk to me. He never seemed rushed.

As a pastor myself, I now realize how busy he really was. When I came unannounced I was interrupting his schedule, taking time he had planned to use in some other way, yet he always graciously took time for me. He saw his time as God's time and he was available to help me work through decisions that are responsible for where I am today.

God has given us time to invest in others. And often that needs to begin at home. Husbands and wives need to invest time in each other and parents need to invest time in their children. The most valuable thing we can give another person is our time.

Then in verse 42 we find the fourth right we need to surrender to be peacemakers, the right to our money. As with our time and possessions, so our money is a stewardship from God. Several years ago I took one of my children to the bank to open a savings account. As we entered the bank the child was perfectly willing to deposit the money, especially since I told my child that the bank would pay interest. Then the child asked me where the bank got the money to pay them interest. I explained that the bank would lend out the money at higher interest. With that the child was not so sure they wanted to deposit the money. Nervously the child asked, "Suppose the person doesn't pay it back?"

I assured the child that the bank was careful about whom they lent money to and it would be paid back. I explained that even if it was not paid back the bank was insured by a government agency. With some misgivings the child did deposit the money.

How often we are like that child of mine with our money. We do not really trust God with it. We want to hold on and manage it ourselves. In fact, it is that holding on, whether it is holding on to our right to retaliate, holding on to our possessions, or holding on to our time, that makes us real losers. It is love that allows us to let go and be peacemakers. And it is peacemakers who are the real winners. Jesus said they will be called the children of God.

That brings us to the third characteristic, loving. In verse 43, Jesus says, "you have heard it said, 'Love your neighbor and hate your enemy.'" Here is a classic example of the Pharisees making their tradition equal to the law. The phrase, "Love your neighbor," comes from the law, but the phrase, "hate your enemies," comes from the tradition of the Pharisees.

The Pharisees had a narrow view of who their neighbors were so they were only obligated to love their friends. That left them free to hate their enemies. However Jesus taught that everyone is our neighbor and that is the intention of the law. Jesus vividly made this point in the parable of the Good Samaritan.

Now talking about loving our enemies can get abstract so let me make it a little more concrete. I want you to picture the person you detest most on this earth, the person who has caused you the most pain and anguish, the person you utterly despise. If there is anyone who can honestly say there is no one like that in their lives, I would like to meet you. For the rest of us who are human, picture that person who has caused you misery. Jesus says we should love them. Anyone can love people who are nice to them. Even nonChristians can do that. But Jesus says to love that person who has hurt us deeply and caused unbearable pain.

Now I can hear some of you thinking, "But you don't know my enemy; no one could ever love them after what they did to me." Let me share two points to help us deal with this. First, we need to remember love is not an emotion. Loving your enemies does not mean having warm feelings for them or enjoying being with them. Love has nothing to do with feelings. Read the Biblical description of love in 1 Corinthians 13, you will not find one feeling or emotion used to define love. In fact, nowhere in the Bible is love ever described as a feeling or an emotion. Love is a behavior. Love is doing the best for another. God never asks us to have warm feelings for someone, he tells us to treat them right.

Imagine a father is sitting on his front porch. He notices his little daughter riding her tricycle down the driveway toward the street. Then he sees a truck coming down the street. There is a row of hedges along the driveway. He realizes the driver will not see his daughter and that his daughter will be hit by the truck. While he has enough time to race from the porch and push his daughter clear, he will probably be struck by the truck. To sacrifice himself for his daughter would be an act of love.

Also imagine a mean little boy who is always teasing his daughter lives on the same street. This boy throws stones at his house and is nasty to his wife. As you can imagine this father has negative feelings toward this mean little boy. Now imagine it is this nasty little boy who is riding down the driveway and into the path of the truck. What do you think the man will do? Without hesitation he runs into the street, reaches the boy in time and pushes him to safety. However the man is struck by the truck. That man acted in love, not on his feelings.

The Bible tells us in Romans 5:8 "God demonstrates his own love for us in this: while we were still enemies Christ died for us." Because God loved us so much while we were still enemies we can love our enemies. In Romans 5:5 the Bible tells us that God sheds his love abroad in our hearts. As believers we can allow God to manifest his love through us.

It may be easier to see how Christianity comes into play in the major crises of life, but what about the hum-drum of everyday routine? In this passage we find three principles we can apply in our everyday lives. The first principle is: Honesty is not the best policy, it is the only policy. We need to be people of integrity. We need to be honest in all we do. Our *yes* is to be *yes* and our *no* is to be *no*.

The second principle is: Peacemakers surrender their rights to win. The paradox is, when we surrender our rights we inherit the Kingdom of God and become his children. We become losers in the world's eyes but winners in God's eyes. Also, look at people who fight for their rights. You do not see smiling faces. That is another paradox, fighting for our rights does not make us happy, it usually makes us miserable.

The third principle is: To love our neighbors we must love our enemies. You see hate destroys, not our enemies, but us. On the other hand love blesses us as well as our enemies. We think our right to revenge, to possessions, to time and to money will make us happy. The reality is defending our rights makes us miserable but surrendering our rights is a source of joy.

Let us move beyond the letter of the law to the spirit of the law and become all God created us to be. We can do it by being people of integrity, peacemakers, and loving. The great part of it is that God enables us to live this way through the Holy Spirit who indwells us. Jesus promised his followers abundant life, let us go for it.

7

How to Talk To God

Matthew 6:1–18

How do we communicate with people we care about? I would like to suggest that there are at least three ways we talk to people we love: with gifts, with words, and with actions. It is very common for us to talk to people we care for with gifts. My wife, Sandy, really likes mums; so one year for our anniversary I gave her a large mums plant. A few years ago Sandy mentioned she would like a gold heart on a gold chain. So for Christmas that year I gave her one. My gifts to her are given to say, "I appreciate you and I love you." We say a great deal with gifts.

Obviously we also talk with words. When Sandy and I were courting we would spend hours in conversation. We still spend quite a bit of time talking. And we talk with our actions. We are all familiar with expressions such as: "Actions speak louder than words," or "What you're doing is speaking so loud I can't hear what you're saying."

Using these three ways of talking to people, with gifts, with words and with actions, I would like to give you suggestions on how to talk to someone you really care about. Think of the person you care for most, someone you really love, a husband, a wife, a boy friend or girl friend, someone really special. These suggestions I am going to share will make you feel even closer to them.

First, do not give that person you love anything you cannot spare or anything you really want for yourself. Only give them leftovers or what you no longer need. Never give them anything you have to sacrifice for. Second, only speak to the person briefly before meals and just before going to bed. Ignore them at all other times. Oh . . . by the way, when you do speak to them, be constantly asking for things. Third, do not ever give up anything for them or go out of your way for them. Only do for them what pleases you.

Wait a minute! Are you crazy? No one would ever treat anyone they really cared about that way. You are right, but that is the way many of us treat our God. We give him what we think we can afford to give. We only speak briefly with God before meals and bed and when we do it is usually to ask for things. We are not willing to give up our sports, recreation and other activities when we have an opportunity to serve him. What are we telling God with our gifts, words, and actions? In Matthew 6:1–18, Jesus tells us how to talk to God.

In verses 1–4, Jesus begins with giving. Maybe that is because we say more to God with our giving than in any other way. Jesus taught that where we put our treasure is the best indicator of where our heart is. "Here we go," you may be thinking, "another lecture on giving." However, in these verses Jesus is not discussing general stewardship, he is talking about giving to the needy or what we call alms. Webster's dictionary defines alms as, ". . . something given freely to relieve the poor." The Greek word comes from a root meaning to show compassion or mercy.

Alms play an important role in Islamic religion. Islam teaches that your good deeds will be weighed against your bad deeds. If your good deeds outweigh your bad deeds you will get into heaven. So whenever Muslims do something bad they need to do something good to offset it. One good deed that earns a great deal of credit is giving alms to the poor. Dr. J. Christy Wilson, in his book on Islam, tells us that giving of alms to the poor was practiced by the prophet Mohammed and continues to be a work of merit. Alms are one of the five pillars of Islam.

The Bible also talks about alms. However the Bible talks about alms or giving to the poor, not as a means of earning merit or salvation, but as an expression of our love for God. And the Bible equates our giving to the poor with our giving to God himself. The Bible teaches in Proverbs 14:31 that oppressing the poor is oppressing God but being generous to the poor is honoring God. Proverbs 19:17 teaches that giving to the poor is lending to God. In Matthew 25:31–46 Jesus talks about feeding the hungry and clothing the naked. Then he says, what we have done for the least of these, we have done for him.

Candidates and politicians are already busy campaigning for the next election. They are, even now, out hunting for votes. A standard campaign ritual is to kiss babies. Why do candidates kiss babies? They cannot vote for another 18 years. They kiss babies, not for the sake of the babies, but for the sake of the parents. When someone is nice to my children they are being nice to me. In the same way, when we are kind to the poor we are being kind to God. When we are generous with the poor we show God we love him.

Then Jesus goes on to tell us the wrong way to give and the right way to give. We are not to give to receive honor from people. We are to give to honor God. Again we find Jesus looking at our inner attitudes as well as our outer behavior.

Not only do we talk to God in our giving, we also talk to God with our words. In verse 5 Jesus tells us how not to talk to God, he says, "And when you pray, do not be like the hypocrites, for they love to pray standing in the synagogues and on the street corners to be seen by people. I tell you the truth, they have received their reward in full." Some people have tried to claim that Jesus is teaching against public prayer. That interpretation misses the whole point. Jesus is teaching that prayer is talking to God and not a ritual to impress others with our piety.

When I was a student at Moody Bible Institute meals were served family style in the dining room. Before we ate one of the deans would say a simple prayer of thanks for the food. If there was a visiting pastor, guest speaker, or other dignitary present at the meal, that person would often be asked to say the prayer. Most of them would say a short, simple prayer. However, from time to time someone would offer a long eloquent prayer to try to impress us. This is what Jesus was talking about. We need to remember that prayer is talking to God.

In verse 7 Jesus speaks against the use of vain repetitions. The other evening I wanted to tell Sandy how much I appreciated her so I said to her: "Oh most glorious and majestic Sandy, it's with great humility that I come into your presence tonight. I would like to express to you, O Sandy, how unworthy I am to be your husband. And, Sandy, you are worthy of all my appreciation. Oh most precious Sandy, it's so good to be able to talk with tonight." Of course I did not talk to her like that. No one talks to real people that way and maybe that is why God does not seem real to us. We need to talk to God like we would a real person.

When I was teaching at St. Paul Bible College, now Crown College, another professor was telling me about when he first met his wife. She was a new believer and did not come from a church background and had not heard people pray before. He said that when she prayed it was like she was talking to someone right in the room with her. Do you want to feel closer to God? Then try talking to him like you would a real person. If we talk to God like we do to real people he will seem more real and personal to us.

Then in verses 9 to 13 Jesus went on to teach his disciples how to pray. Now, I do not believe Jesus shared this prayer with his disciples as a prayer to be repeated or recited, but, rather, as a model. If it was meant to be a model, then we should study it for its structure rather than its specific content. We find five elements in this prayer.

The first element is God's person. We need to tell God what we think of him and how much we care for him. What should we say? Try listening to children. When my children say to me, "You're the greatest," or "I'm glad you're my dad," or "I love you," it makes me feel great. All we need to do is to be natural, open, and honest.

The second element is God's program. Most of us are quick to acknowledge God as Savior but slow to acknowledge him as Lord. We need to tell God we are ready to follow his program. The third element is God's provision. When my children were young and lived at home they constantly asked for things. Some they got, some they did not. But they kept asking because they knew I loved them and I would give them what was good for them. They did not just ask for big things, they also asked for little things. Sometimes they even asked for things for their friends. Jesus said we were to come to God in prayer as our Father. Enough said, I am sure you get the point.

The fourth element is God's purity. Because God is holy he cannot tolerate sin. But he has made a provision for our sin. In 1 Timothy 2:5–6 the Bible tells us, "For there is one God and one mediator between God and us, the man Christ Jesus who gave himself as a ransom for everyone." And the Bible tells us in 1 John 1:9, "If we confess our sins [God] is faithful and just to forgive our sins and cleanse us from all unrighteousness."

There are three keys to dealing with sin in our lives. The first is confession, admitting to God that we have sinned. The second is restitution, making right anything we have done wrong. Jesus taught in Matthew 5:23–24, that if we approach God and then remember that someone has something against us, we are to go make it right first and then approach

God. The third is renunciation, we are to renounce our sin or turn from it, what the Bible calls repentance.

By the way, the Bible clearly teaches that if we have unconfessed sin in our lives God will not listen to our prayers. In Isaiah 59:1–2 we read, "Surely the arm of the Lord is not too short to save, nor his ear to dull to hear. But your iniquities have separated you from your God: your sins have hidden his face from you so that he will not hear." Psalm 66:18 says, "If I had cherished sin in my heart the Lord would not have listened. . . ." And in Proverbs 28:9 we read, "If anyone turns a deaf ear to the law even his prayers are detestable." Dealing with sin is the key to open communication with God.

The fifth element is God's protection. The Bible tells us in 1 John 4:4, "You, dear children, are from God and have overcome [the evil one] because the one who is in you is greater than the one who is in the world." And the Bible tells us in Romans 8:31 and 37, "If God is for us who can be against us? . . . No, in all these things we are more than conquerors through him who loves us."

Now there is a critical issue in verses 12, 14, and 15 that we need to discuss. There we read, "Forgive us our debts as we have also forgiven our debtors. . . . For if you forgive people when they sin against you, your heavenly Father will also forgive you. But if you do not forgive people their sins, your Father will not forgive your sins."

Taken literally these verses are quite troubling. They seem to say that God will only forgive us if we forgive others. However, we know that the Bible teaches that forgiveness is by grace and not by works. So that cannot be the correct interpretation. Well, then, what do these verses mean?

I consulted several commentaries on these verses and I could not find a satisfactory answer. Some commentaries literally avoided these verses and others double-talked their way around them. In Ephesians 4:32 we read, "And be kind to one another, tender-hearted, forgiving each other just as God in Christ has also forgiven you." This verse gives us a possible explanation. Notice our forgiving others follows God's forgiving us. If we are not willing to forgive others then we may not have truly received God's forgiveness. God's forgiveness is not dependent on our works, but it is dependent on our repentance. The evidence that we have truly been forgiven is that we can forgive others. While we may not be able to fully explain these verses we should have no trouble obeying them. The command is clear: we are to forgive others.

And this brings us to our third way of talking to God, through our actions. One such action is fasting. "What exactly is fasting?" you may ask. Fasting is abstaining from food for a specified period of time to focus on God. Fasting is not a form of works. It does not get prayers answered sooner or prayers answered that otherwise would not get answered. It is a spiritual discipline to help us focus on God.

In verse 16 Jesus tells us how not to fast. He says fasting is not to be engaged in as a public ritual. Fasting should be done for God, not for public recognition. Then, in verses 17 and 18, Jesus tells us how to fast. He says to do it as a personal dedication to God. In the Bible fasting is generally associated with prayer and/or worship. I know many believers who make it a practice to fast one day a week and spend the extra time in prayer. While Jesus is dealing with fasting in these verses, there is a larger principle that can be applied to all our actions. They should be done for God, not for public recognition.

As we apply the passage we have studied together to our lives, I would like to ask three questions and then make three suggestions. We will begin with the three questions. The first is: What am I saying to God with my giving? The second is: What am I saying to God with my words? The third is: What am I saying to God with my actions? You see, we are always talking to God, the real question is: what are we saying to him?

Let me share three suggestions for improving our communication with God. First, tell God you love him by your generosity. One way is by caring for the needy. There are several practical ways to do that. One way is through your church's benevolent offering. Another is to reach out directly to a needy family. You might drop off groceries at the home of a needy person. Give to or volunteer at food shelf. Donate used clothes and furniture to the Salvation Army. There are many ways to help the needy.

Another way we can tell God we love him is by bringing our tithe for his work. God has told us to bring 10% of our income, a tithe, for his work. The Bible tells us in Malachi 3:6–10 that when we withhold our tithe we are robbing God. No one robs someone they really love.

The second suggestion is: talk to God like you would a real person and do it often. You will be amazed at how real he will seem and how close you will feel to him. Talk to him about how much you love him. Thank him for all he has done for you. And bring your needs and concerns to him.

The third suggestion is: talk to God with your actions. Make sacrifices for him, sacrifices of time, sacrifices of things, sacrifices of money, sacrifices of meals, not to win his favor, but to tell him you love him.

I would like to share the true story of Brother Demetrius. He was an Eastern Orthodox priest ministering in the Middle East. He had a special gift for teaching people to enrich their lives through prayer. He cared very deeply for the people of his village and was much loved by them.

One day a tragic riot occurred in the village causing extensive damage. One family lost all its possessions, the family dwelling, furniture, clothing, and business were all destroyed. Friends and relatives came to their assistance including Brother Demetrius. He volunteered to help the youngest daughter. Brother Demetrius did not have much money, but he took what he had and bought the girl shoes, a dress and a coat. And he also bought her a pretty ring.

The people of the village began to talk, they said, "He's such a good and loving man, but it was foolish of him to buy a ring when she had so many other needs." When Brother Demetrius heard this talk he quietly responded, "I wanted to give her things that would remind her not only of her poverty, but also to help her know she is loved."

How do we tell God we love him? In the Bible Mary did it by pouring expensive perfume on Jesus. Some also saw that as a waste but Jesus saw it as an expression of love. Are we telling God that we love Him?

8

Where Is Your Treasure?

Matthew 6:19–34

A WHILE BACK I came across the story of a woman who bought a parrot to keep her company. The next day she returned to the pet store and complained that the parrot did not speak. "Does he have a mirror in his cage?" asked the store owner. "Parrots love mirrors. They see their reflection and start talking." So the woman bought a mirror and left.

The next day she returned to the pet store complaining that the parrot still did not speak. "How about a ladder?" asked the owner. "Parrots love to climb and a happy parrot is a talkative parrot." So the woman bought a ladder.

But the following day she was back again, the parrot still was not talking. "Does your parrot have a swing?" asked the owner. The woman told him the parrot did not have a swing. "Well, there's your problem," said the owner, "Once he starts swinging he'll talk up a storm." The woman reluctantly bought a swing and left.

She returned to the pet store the next day and sadly explained that the parrot had died. The owner was shocked and expressed his sorrow. He asked the woman if the parrot had ever said a word. "Yes," replied the woman, "Just before he died, he asked in a weak voice, 'Don't they sell any food at that pet store?'"

Sometimes we are like that woman we focus on everything except what is really important. We accumulate all the bells and whistles and miss the essentials. The Emperor Napoleon seized control of Spain in 1808. He forced Ferdinand VII to resign the Spanish throne. Then Napoleon placed his brother, Joseph, on the throne. They threw Ferdinand into solitary confinement in Madrid's notorious Navy Prison, the Place of the Skull. Ferdinand, who had lived the pampered life of a king, suddenly found himself in a single room filled with filth and rodents. He was allowed to bring with him only one personal possession, a Bible. For almost seven years that Bible was Ferdinand's only break from the monotony of his cell. He read through the Bible hundreds of times.

He was freed from prison in 1814 and returned to his throne. Meanwhile, his jailors found in his cell a curious collection of Bible notes and comments. With a small piece of metal he'd scratched on the walls of his cell the results of years of Bible study. On every surface there were hundreds of comments such as:

> There are 33,214 verses in the Bible.
> There are 774,746 words in the Bible.
> There are 838,380 letters in the New Testament.
> Ezra 7:21 contains every letter of the alphabet except *j*.
> Esther 8:9 is the longest verse in the Bible.
> John 11:35 is the shortest verse in the Bible.

What a tragedy! Ferdinand had the unique opportunity to study the Word of God for almost seven years and all he got out of his time were lists of trivia. We may think that Ferdinand had his priorities all wrong, but what about us? In Matthew 6:19–34, Jesus discusses our priorities. In this passage Jesus says our priorities and values are revealed by our choices. Then he lays out four choices that reveal our true values.

When we move to a new community we have to find a place to do our banking. We look for a bank that is conveniently located and is competitive with other banks. While we have to find a bank to handle our finances, we also have to find a bank to handle our eternal treasures.

The first choice, Jesus says, that reveals our true values is where we bank our eternal treasures: in the bank of the world or in the bank of heaven? In verse 19 Jesus points out the transient nature of earthly possessions and in verse 20 the permanent nature of treasure invested in heaven. Then in verse 20 Jesus says, "For where your treasure is, there your heart will be also." As most of you know, in the cultures of the Bible, the heart did not represent the seat of the emotions, but, rather the seat of the will.

What Jesus is saying, is our choices, that is, our values and priorities, will be determined by where we put our treasure.

This leads to a question: how do I store up treasure in heaven? The unique thing about the bank of heaven is, it only takes deposits in advance, you cannot take it with you. I like what I heard Chuck Swindoll once say, "I've never seen a hearse pulling a U-Haul trailer."

Now there are three types of deposits that can be made in the bank of heaven. The first is money. There are two ways we deposit money in the bank of heaven. The first is tithes. The Bible clearly teaches that 10% of our income, the tithe, belongs to God. In fact that is why the Bible does not say to give the tithe, it says to bring it. We cannot give it because it is not ours, and when we do not bring it God says we are robbing him (Malachi 3:6–12). The tithe is not the end of Biblical stewardship; it is the beginning point.

That brings us to the second type of money deposit we can make in the bank of heaven, offerings. Offerings are gifts given for God's work above and beyond the tithe. The collections Paul discusses in his second letter to the church at Corinth were offerings for the poor above the tithe. Offerings are to be proportional to how God has blessed us; the more we have been blessed the more we should give. The Bible tells us in Deuteronomy 16:17, "Each of you must bring a gift in proportion to the way the Lord God has blessed you."

The second type of deposit we can make in the bank of heaven is time. We can invest our time for the Kingdom of God. The Bible teaches that each of us, as believers, has been given at least one spiritual gift, that is a ministry ability from the Holy Spirit, to use in ministry in the body of Christ, the church. Have you found a place of ministry in the church? Are you investing your time in God's work?

The third and most important type of deposit we can make in the bank of heaven is ourselves. Over in the first five verses of 2 Corinthians 8, we read, "And now, brothers, we want you to know about the grace God has given the Macedonian churches. Out of the most severe trial, their overflowing joy and their extreme poverty welled up in rich generosity. For I testify they gave as much as they were able, and even beyond their ability. Entirely on their own, they urgently pleaded with us for the privilege of sharing in this service to the saints. And they did not do as we expected, but they gave themselves first to the Lord and then to us in keeping with God's will."

Did you catch that last part? They gave themselves first. The secret to depositing in the bank of heaven is to give ourselves first. "How do we do that?" you ask. We turn everything we have and are over to God. We put God in control of all our finances, all our possessions, all our resources, all our time, all we are. The reality is, it is all His anyway, we are not really giving anything away. But when we turn control over to God, He gives us His best.

When my children were little and they had something that was valuable to them, they would often turn it over to me. They knew that if they held onto it, it would get broken or lost but if I had it, it would be safe. If my children could trust me with their most valuable possessions, how much more can we trust our heavenly Father? Which bank are you using? Where are you storing your treasure?

The second choice Jesus says we have is how we will look at life. In verses 22 and 23 Jesus says the eye of our soul can be either clear or dirty. When we lived in Wisconsin we would go through bottles of windshield washer fluid every spring. All winter long the snow would keep accumulating. Then in the spring, as the days warmed, the snow would begin to melt. This left the roads wet. The spray from the wheels of other cars and trucks quickly covered our cars with dirt. Driving around that time of year we had to be constantly using our windshield washer to clean the grime off the windshield.

As we drive through life the grime of the world dirties the eye of our soul, it darkens our spiritual vision. Now, driving around Wisconsin in the spring you cannot just clean your windshield once and expect it to stay clean. You need to clean your windshield regularly. In the same way we need to come to Christ for regular spiritual cleansing.

The epistle of 1 John was written to believers and in chapter 1, verse 9, we read, "If we confess our sins [God] is faithful and just to forgive us our sins and cleanse us from all unrighteousness." As believers we do sin, we do fail, but God has made provision for us. As the bumper sticker says, "Christians aren't perfect, just forgiven." The church is not a country club for perfect people; it is a first-aid station for sinners. And I am so glad it is, if only the perfect could be involved, if only those who have it all together spiritually are welcome, then I could not be there. But God wants us to deal with our sin, to clean up our vision. How do we do that?

There are three ways to deal with sin in our lives. The first way is confession. We need to admit to God that we have sinned, that we have failed.

And we need to ask for His forgiveness. The second way is restitution, we need to make it right. If we have offended someone we need to apologize. If we have lied to someone we need to set it straight. Whatever we have done, we need to make it right. The third way is we need to change. We need to ask God to help us overcome that sin. We need to allow the Holy Spirit to work in our lives to bring about change. We need to keep our spiritual vision clear.

The third choice we face, the one that ultimately affects the others, is the choice of a master. Historically there have been two ways in which one became a slave, by being captured or sold. In either case a person does not choose his or her master. In verse 24 Jesus says we can choose between God and money. The Greek word is *mammon* which is a transliteration of a Hebrew word. That means the word was brought from the Hebrew language into Greek. The Hebrew word is made from two root words. One is the root word for *wealth* and the other is the root word for *trust*. So the word means to trust in wealth. For the Hebrews wealth meant more than just money, it also referred to all material possessions. Jesus says we have a choice of a master, God or wealth.

There are two ways to choose God as our master. The first is by faith. Are we going to trust God or trust wealth? It often amazes me how believers are able to trust God with their eternal destiny but not with their present lives. If we really believed that God loves us and wants the best for us, we would have no trouble trusting Him with our lives and our possessions.

The second way we choose God is by action. The Apostle James writes that faith without works is dead. If God is our master we should be obeying him. Our actions are the ultimate proof of who our master really is. By the way, if you think you can be your own master you are only fooling yourself. Each of us will serve someone or something. There is only one Master that loves us and wants the best for us.

And that leads to our fourth choice, the choice between worry and faith. You see, when we choose to serve wealth we have to worry, because, as Jesus said, it rusts, decays and gets stolen. Or to put it in contemporary terms, the stock market crashes, the housing market weakens, interest rates are unstable, and job security is nonexistent.

In verses 25 and 26 Jesus says worry is irrelevant. It is interesting to note that in the Bible all human emotions are attributed to God; anger, joy, disappointment, grief, all human emotions except worry and fear. Why does Jesus say worry is irrelevant? Because it cannot change anything. If you worry about something and it happens your worry did not help. If it does not happen your worrying was wasted. In either case worry is useless.

Third, in verses 31–34, Jesus says worry is irresponsible. Jesus says that our responsibility, as His followers, is to seek the Kingdom of God and His righteousness. Our responsibility is to trust God with our needs so worry is irresponsible. Jesus teaches us to replace worry with faith. As we replace worry with faith we need to realize there are three things faith does not do.

First, faith does not exempt us from work. Faith is trusting God to guide us and enable us to do what has to be done. Faith is not expecting God to do it for us. We have to work, but He is there with us. When my children were in grade school they would sometimes come and ask me to help them with their homework. I did not say, "You go out and play and I'll finish it for you." Rather I sat down with them and did it with them. But they still had to work. Faith is not based on works but real faith produces works. The Bible tells us in James 2:26, "As the body without the spirit is dead so faith without works is dead."

The second thing faith does not do is exempt us from helping others. In James 2:15–17 we read, "Suppose a brother or sister is without clothes and daily food. If one of you says to them, 'Go, I wish you well; keep warm and well fed,' but does nothing about their physical needs, what good is it? In the same way, faith by itself, if not accompanied by action is dead."

Real faith does not just pray for sick friend; it brings a meal by and visits. Real faith does not just pray for a family where the husband is out of work; it stops by with a bag of groceries. Real faith does not just pray for a new widow or widower; it invites them over for dinner. Real faith does not just pray for church growth, it invites people to church.

The third thing faith does not do is exempt us from trouble. We live in a sin-ravished world. Pain, grief, sickness, and death are the lot of the Christian as well as the unsaved. Worry does not help when trouble comes, but faith does. God did not promise us a trouble-free life, but He did promise to go with us through our troubles.

We have looked at what faith does not do, but what does it do? First, it seeks God's Kingdom. How do we seek God's kingdom? By faith. The Bible tells us that all who want to come to God must believe that He is and that He rewards those who seek Him. We come into the Kingdom of God by faith in Jesus Christ.

Second, Jesus taught that faith does seek God's righteousness. Again righteousness comes by faith. The Bible tells us that Abraham believed God and God counted it as righteousness. We have a choice, we can sit around and worry or we can exercise faith. And we need to realize that faith is active not passive. Take your Bible and look at Hebrews, chapter 11, and you will see what an active faith looks like.

As we seek to apply what we have studied let me leave you with four questions. The first is: where am I banking? What am I investing in, the things of the world or the things of heaven? Remember, in the bank of heaven you can only make deposits in advance. The second question is: what am I doing about sin? Are our spiritual eyes dirty with sin or are we cleaning them regularly with confession, restitution, and change? The third question is: who am I serving? As Jesus said, we cannot serve two masters. Now, I am sure most of us would claim we serve God. But what does our behavior show? As someone has said, two books will show where our values really are, our check book and our date book. Where are we investing our money and time? The fourth question is: how am I thinking? Are my thoughts filled with worry or faith?

In her book, *Teaching a Stone to Talk*, Annie Dillard tells about the ill-fated Franklin expedition of 1845. The explorers sailed from England to find the Northwest Passage across the Arctic Ocean. They took aboard their two sailing ships a lot of things they did not need including: a 1,200-volume library, fine china, crystal goblets, and other luxuries. Amazingly each ship took only a 12-day supply of coal for their auxiliary steam engines. The ships became trapped in vast frozen plains of ice. After several months Lord Franklin died. The men decided to trek to safety in small groups, none survived.

One story is especially revealing. Two officers pulled a large sled more than 65 miles across treacherous ice. When rescuers found their bodies they found the sled filled with table silver and other valuables. Because they tried to keep the treasure they lost their lives. Those men made a choice and they lived and died with the consequences of their choice.

Today we are confronted with a series of choices and we will live and die with the consequences of our choices. Actually the choices really boil down to one, who is going to be in charge of our lives? When we put Jesus Christ in charge as our Lord he enables us to become all we were created to be and to accomplish all we were created to do.

9

Eyewash, Pigs, and Dogs

Matthew 7:1–6

"THE BRITISH ARE COMING!" "The British are coming!" The cry rang through the hot August afternoon air. The British Army was on the move, advancing rapidly. They were searching for a single man, the leader of the rebellion. The rebellion against British rule had been growing. Those opposing King George consisted of a small but courageous band of patriots. And their leader needed to be found. He had not listened when his men warned him that the British were coming. Now he woke up to the sound of a barking dog in the front yard. He heard the clatter of British troops approaching in the distance. The leader of the revolution made his way quickly to the attic and hid in a secret compartment that had been prepared for him.

The town was surrounded and the British soldiers began a house-to-house search. When the soldiers arrived at the house where the leader of the revolution was hiding, the woman of the house let them in. The soldiers searched the house from top to bottom but could not find anything. However they took the woman and her two small children into custody.

The patriot leader lay in his sweltering tomb, trapped in the ceiling of the house, as the hot August sun beat down on the roof. Without food or water, he realized that he could be left to die in that unmarked tomb. However woman was released by the British, she freed the leader of the revolution, and the dream of a new nation survived. He went on to lead the revolutionary forces to victory, eventually becoming the leader of his country.

The time? 1776? The British King? King George the Third? The patriot? George Washington? That was my conclusion when I heard the story from Paul Harvey. Was it yours as you read it? Well here is the rest of the story. It turns out the year was 1946 and the British King was King George the Seventh. The patriot leader was Menachem Begin and the new country was the State of Israel.

Following the destruction of Jerusalem in AD 70 the Jewish people were scattered throughout the Roman Empire. Palestine remained under Roman rule until the 4th Century. It was then ruled by the Byzantine Empire until 632 when it was captured by Muslim Arabs. In 1517 Palestine was conquered by the Turkish Ottoman Empire. Palestine remained under Turkish rule until the First World War. During the First World War Turkey sided with Germany and Austria against the allies.

When the Allies won the war, Palestine passed into their hands. In 1917 France and Britain signed the Balfor Declaration which called for the establishment of a national homeland for the Jewish people while preserving the rights of existing non-Jewish communities (what today are the Palestinians). It also gave Britain control over Palestine and European Jews poured into Palestine.

In 1917 there were about 50,00 Jews in Palestine, by 1939 the Jewish population was half a million. With the outbreak of World War II Jewish migration to Palestine was reduced to a trickle. When the war ended hundreds of thousands of Jewish refugees sought to migrate to Palestine. The British, who ruled Palestine, sought to limit this Jewish immigration to appease the Arabs. The book, *Exodus*, by Leon Uris, and the movie based on the book, deal with the efforts of European Jews to migrate to Palestine, and the British effort to stop them.

Britain, under a UN mandate, sought to partition Palestine into two states, one Jewish and one Palestinian. The Jews wanted all of Palestine, their historic homeland, for a Jewish state. Jewish revolutionary movements such as Haganah, lead by Ben Gurion, and Irgun, lead by Menachem Begin, fought the British. In 1948 Britain pulled out of Palestine and Israel declared itself a sovereign state. In 1977 Menachem Begin was elected Prime Minister of Israel.

The story of Menachem Begin's escape from the British soldiers demonstrates how easy it is for us to jump to false conclusions. If you are like me, you thought it was the American revolution and the leader was George Washington. But we were wrong.

The passage we are studying in this chapter, Matthew 7:1-6, deals with Jesus' teaching on jumping to conclusions or judging. This is a very difficult passage in general and verse 6 is particularly difficult. I have wrestled with this passage for some time and believe I am beginning to understand the point Jesus is making. In verses 1–5 Jesus is teaching that we are not to judge fellow believers, while in verse 6 he is teaching we are to judge unbelievers in our midst.

Before we look at these verses in detail let me remind you that the Sermon on the Mount was not addressed to the multitudes, it was addressed to Jesus' disciples, his followers. Also we need to keep this passage in the context of the Sermon on the Mount which deals with the Kingdom of God.

A pastor was visiting one of his parishioners and as they were talking the lady pointed out her window to her neighbor's backyard where the wash was hanging. The woman commented, "See that lady next door, her wash is always dirty." The pastor was uncomfortable with the turn in conversation and attempted to change the subject. He asked the woman to show him her garden, explaining he had heard so much about it. As they walked out the backdoor the neighbor's wash was clearly visible to them. The pastor and the woman both realized at the same time that the wash was sparkling white. The truth began to dawn on them; it was not the neighbor's wash that was dirty, it was the woman's windows.

Here, in verses 1–5, Jesus talks about our need to clean our own eye before we look at others. He begins verse 1 by saying, "Do not judge. . . ." Every commentary I consulted attempted to water down this command. They all had exceptions to it. However I do not believe there are any exceptions. I believe Jesus meant what he said.

In verses 3, 4, and 5 he uses the word *brother*. Since Jesus was addressing his disciples, what he is saying is, believers should not judge each other. This command is simple and straightforward; we are not to judge each other—ever!

The Apostle Paul tells us the same thing in Romans 14:4, where he writes, "Who are you to judge the servant of another?" And then he adds in verse 13, "Therefore let us not judge each other anymore." The Bible tells us in James 4:11, "Do not speak against one another, brethren. He who speaks against his brother or judges his brother speaks against the law. . . ."

Now, I can see a question beginning to form in some of your minds: "If believers are never to judge each other, what do we do about another believer living in sin?" I am glad you raised that question because I am going to answer it in a moment. But first I want to look at three reasons Jesus gave for not judging each other.

First, we are not qualified. In verses 1 and 2 Jesus tells us if we judge other believers we will be judged. Who will judge us? The true judge, the only judge. The Bible tells us in James 4:12, "There is only one Lawgiver and Judge, the One who is able to save and destroy." And the Apostle Paul writes in Romans 14:10, "Why do you judge your brother? For we shall all stand before the judgment seat of God." God is the only one qualified to judge believers because he is omniscient. He knows all the facts. When we try to judge on limited knowledge we are often wrong.

When my sister and I were growing up we used to tease each other and fight like most brothers and sisters. We would also, at times, take perverse delight in getting each other in trouble. Sometimes my sister would cry and say I had hit her even when I had not, just to get me in trouble. Because I did hit her at times, when she did cry and pretend I had hit her, I would get in trouble. My parents were not omniscient and they judged the situation wrongly.

One time my sister was mad at me about something and to get even she started to scream that I hit her. What she did not know was that my father was standing in the doorway behind her. After that, even when I really hit my sister, they did not believe her. Again they judged wrongly. Now parents are to judge between their children even though their judgment will be imperfect, but believers are not to judge each other.

I knew a pastor who was accused of sexual immorality based on circumstantial evidence. He was driven from his pulpit and eventually into a mental hospital. When all the facts came out, it turned out he had not done anything wrong. That faulty judging split a church and wrecked a ministry. My wife and I were involved in helping pick up the pieces. When we judge without knowing all the facts we may be wrong. And our wrong judgment can cause others heartache and pain. Since we can never know all the facts, we are never in a position to judge other believers.

The second reason Jesus says we are not to judge other believers, is: we are not impartial. In verse 3, Jesus says, "Why do you look at the speck of sawdust in your brother's eye and pay no attention to the plank in your own eye." The word *plank* is actually a specific term for a beam that would hold up the roof of a house. The *speck* is actually a tiny splinter from the same wood. In the original language the log and the splinter are from the same source. What Jesus is saying is that the sin in the other person's life is the same as in yours, but you have got more of it.

What I am going to say now may not be too popular or well received, but I believe it is the essence of what Jesus is teaching. You will recall when we studied Matthew chapter 5, that Jesus took the Pharisees to task for living by the letter of the law while ignoring the spirit of the law. The Pharisees were only concerned with outward behavior and ignored inner attitudes. But Jesus taught that hate was as bad as murder and lust as bad as adultery. Now, do we really believe that?

Let me suggest what Jesus means by the plank and the speck. Here is a woman who has lusted after several men judging a woman she thinks had an affair with one man. Which is the greater sin? Lusting after several people or having an affair with one person? Which is the plank and which is the speck? Do we really believe what Jesus said?

Psychologists have discovered that humans use defense mechanisms to protect themselves from unpleasant thoughts or convictions. One of those defense mechanisms is called projection. It involves a person projecting or attributing their thoughts and motives to another person. For example, if I am doing something for the wrong reason, I assume others are doing it for the wrong reason. I project my motives on them. The truth is, we usually judge harshest in others what is wrong in our own lives. Therefore, when we are tempted to judge another believer, we better examine our own lives in that area.

The third reason Jesus said that we are not to judge others is: we are not good enough. As Jesus points out in verses 4 and 5, we have enough to take care of in our own lives and are in no position to judge others. Only God can judge because only God is completely holy. We are not in a position to judge each other.

In fact, the Bible tells us in 1 Corinthians 11:28–32 that the only believer we are authorized to judge is ourselves. There we read, "But let a person examine themselves . . . if we judged ourselves rightly we would not be judged." We have too much to judge in ourselves to judge others.

But back to the question that was raised earlier. What do we do when it appears another believer is living in open sin? Are we to just ignore it? The Bible gives us clear instructions for those situations. There are two courses of action we are to take. The first is found in Matthew 18:15–17.

There we find three steps in confronting sin. The first step is: go only to the person. Verse 15 says, "If your brother sins against you, go show him his fault, just between the two of you." The earliest manuscripts of the New Testament do not have the words *against you*. They just say *if your brother sins*.

The key is, we are to go directly to the person we believe is sinning. Why? Because maybe after hearing the whole story we may realize we were wrong. The teaching is clear: we only go to the other person. If we discuss it with anyone else, we are sinning. How would you like it if someone thought you were sinning and was talking to other people?

Now, if after talking with the person, you still believe he or she is sinning, you go to step two. The second step is: take one or two others with you. Verse 16 says, "But if he will not listen, take one or two others along, so that 'every matter may be established by the testimony of two or three witnesses.'" Now, the purpose of taking others with us is not to gang up on the person but to establish the facts. The others may determine that you have it all wrong and the other person is right. However, if all of you believe the person is sinning you go to step three.

The third step is: take it to the church leadership. In this case the church leadership may need to exercise church discipline for the good of the individual and the church. However, in each step, including church discipline, the purpose and goal is restoration.

And that leads to the second course of action, which is found in Galatians 6:1, the ministry of restoration. There we read, "Brothers, if someone is caught in a sin, you who are spiritual should restore him gently. But watch yourself or you also may be tempted." We find four insights for the ministry of restoration in this verse.

First we see: this is a ministry for those who are spiritual. This is a ministry for those who are dealing with the sin in their lives and walking with the Lord. If we are not dealing with the sin in our lives we have no business dealing with sin in someone else's life. Second we see: this is a ministry of restoration. This is not a ministry of judging or condemning; it is a ministry of grace and love. Third we see: this is a ministry to be carried out gently. It is not to be done harshly or severely. The goal is not punishment but restoration.

Fourth we see: this is a ministry for those who recognize their own weakness. The person who thinks they could never commit that sin is not qualified for this ministry. This ministry is for those who recognize their weakness and can emphasize with the fallen brother or sister. As believers we have been called to minister to each other, to love each other, to encourage each other, and when necessary to confront each other and restore each other. We have not been called to judge each other, that is God's job.

After telling us not to judge other believers Jesus moves on to talking about dogs and pigs in verse 6. At first glance verse 6 does not seem to fit with what precedes or follows. But a closer look at verse 6 reveals it is related to the first five verses. In the first five verses of this chapter Jesus tells us not to judge other believers. Now, in verse 6, he tells us who to judge.

To the Jews both dogs and pigs were unclean animals. While we keep dogs as pets, the Jews saw dogs as filthy scavengers equivalent to rats. The Jews referred to apostate Jews as dogs and pigs. Here Jesus is using the term to refer to those who have been exposed to the gospel and come into the church but are not true believers. In 2 Peter 2:1 and 22 the Bible says, "But there will be false prophets among the people, just as there will be false prophets among you. They will secretly introduce destructive heresies. . . . Of them the Proverbs are true: 'A dog returns to its vomit,' and 'A pig that is washed goes back to her wallowing in the mud.'"

There are at least two reasons why we are to judge nonChristians in our midst who pretend to be believers. The first is to protect the church from being led astray. This is discussed in more detail in Matthew 7:13–23. We will be looking that passage together in a later chapter. The second reason is to protect the church from sin. The Bible discusses the problems and sins false believers can bring into a congregation. We will also look at that Scripture when we look at Matthew 7:13–23. Our focus in this chapter is on Jesus' teaching that, we as believers, are not to judge each other.

A while back I read about a lady who had lived in a community for many years and was a long-time member of the church. One Sunday morning, as she was shaking hands with the pastor after the service, she said, "That was a wonderful sermon. Everything you said applies to someone I know."

We should not be like that lady rather we should apply these truths to our own lives. So to help us do that, I will leave us with four thoughts. First, we must obey Christ and not judge other believers. Actually, this is not a suggestion; it is a command from Jesus himself. There are no exceptions.

Second, when we are tempted to judge another believer, we should carefully examine our own lives in that area. We need to be careful we are not projecting our sin onto someone else. Our tendency is to judge harshest in others what we are struggling with in our own lives.

Third, if we really believe another believer is sinning we should follow the steps in Matthew 18:15–17. And the first step is the most critical one: we are only to go to the person we think may be sinning. Unfortunately our first inclination is often to go to anyone and everyone other than the person. Jesus tells us to only go to that person.

Fourth, if another believer has fallen into sin, we should work to restore them. In the Bible the only person commissioned to convict people of sin is the Holy Spirit. Convicting people of sin is the Spirit's job and he does not need our help. We have been commissioned to minister to each other and that is our job and the Holy Spirit will help us.

Now you may be thinking, "It sounds like you're soft on sin." However that is not true, I believe we need to be hard on sin, the sin in our lives. But when we deal with others we need to give them the benefit of the doubt. We are part of a culture that has taught us to assume the worst of each other but we can change that. We can begin to assume the best about each other.

Everything I have shared can be summarized in one word: *love*! If we love each other we will not judge each other. If we love each other we will be willing to go to each other if we think something is amiss. If we love each other we will seek to gently restore each other when we fall. Brothers and sister let love one another.

10

Beggars Welcome

Matthew 7:7–12

A WHILE BACK I came across a story about a small Kentucky town that had two churches and one bar. Members of both churches complained that the bar had a bad influence on the community. To make matters worse, the man who owned the bar was an avowed atheist. Failing to close the bar down by legal means the two churches decided to hold a joint prayer meeting. They would ask God to intervene. The night of the prayer meeting there was a severe thunderstorm. As the prayer meeting ended lightening struck the bar and it burned to the ground. The next Sunday the sermons in both churches were on the power of prayer.

Meanwhile the bar owner called his insurance company and they sent out a claims adjuster. When the claims adjuster had gathered all the facts he told the bar owner that the insurance company would not pay his claim. The claims adjuster explained that the policy specifically excluded acts of God.

Then the bar owner turned around and sued all the church members who were at the prayer meeting. He claimed they had conspired with God to destroy his building. The church members denied they had done anything to cause the fire. As the case went to trial the judge observed, "I find this case very confusing. We have a plaintiff, who claims to be an atheist, professing belief in the power of prayer, and defendants, all of whom are church members, denying the power of prayer."

The Bible tells us about another group of church members who denied the power of prayer, not in words but in actions. The account is recorded for us in Acts, chapter 12. The chapter opens with Herod, the local ruler, harassing the Christians in order to win favor with the Jews. Herod had James, the brother of John, publicly executed. When he saw how well that went over with the Jewish leaders he decided to execute Peter also. He had Peter arrested but it was Passover so he had to wait for the religious days to end before he could execute him. The night before the execution an angel came and rescued Peter from prison.

Meanwhile the believers had gathered at the home of Mary, the mother of John Mark, to pray for Peter's release. Peter, found himself free and went to the home to bring the good news that he had been freed. Peter arrived at the house and knocked on the door. Now Christians were not too popular in Jerusalem at that time so the house was locked up tight.

A servant girl named Rhoda went to answer the door. In the door was a little peephole one could open to see who was there. When she opened the little peep door and saw Peter she became so excited she forgot to let him in. She just rushed back to tell the others the good news. What was their response to the news their prayers had been answered? They told Rhoda she was crazy. How do you like that? There they are, all praying for Peter's release, and when someone tells them that their prayer has been answered and he has been released, they say she is crazy.

But, before we are too hard on those early believers, what about us? When we bring our requests to God in prayer do we really believe he will answer us? As we continue our study of the Sermon on the Mount we have come to a passage, Matthew 7:7–12, that deals with prayer and answers to prayer.

As we look at these verses the first thing we find is a command. We are told, in verse 7, to ask, to seek, and to knock. In other words we are told to bring our needs to God in prayer. Let me make two points about this. First, we do not have because we do not ask. The Bible tells us in James 4:2, "You do not have because you do not ask God."

I do not know what problems you face today, I do not know what cares are weighing you down, I cannot see the pain and grief you are bearing. I do not know your fears and aspirations. But I do know there is a command for you in this passage. We are told to ask, to seek, and to knock. By the way, this command is in the Greek present tense, which indicates a continuous action, so it means keep on asking, keep on seeking, and keep on knocking.

The second point is: we can bring everything to God in prayer. The Bible tells us in Philippians 4:6, "Do not be anxious for anything, but in everything, by prayer and petition, with thanksgiving, present your requests to God." God tells us to bring everything to him. There is nothing too small or nothing too big to bring to God in prayer.

Jesus does not just give us a command; he also gives us a promise. In verse 8 we read, "For everyone who asks receives; those who seek find; and to those who knock the door will be opened." Now for some of you these words must seem like a mockery. You have been asking God for something. You have been seeking and knocking but the heavens seem like brass. No answers come, you do not receive, no one opens.

How do we explain these seemingly unanswered prayers in light of Jesus' promise? I would like to share with you six reasons or explanations for unanswered prayers. The first is not coming in faith. The Bible tells us in Hebrews 11:6, "Those who come to God must believe that he is and that he is a rewarder of those who seek him."

And the Bible tells us in James 1:6, "When we ask we must believe and not doubt." How much faith do we need? Jesus taught that we can move mountains with faith as small as a mustard seed. You see, it is not our faith that makes things happen, it is the One we have faith in who makes things happen. God is ready to hear and answer our prayers but we must come in faith.

The second reason our prayers are not answered is we come with the wrong motives. The Bible tells us in James 4:3, "When you ask you do not receive because you ask with wrong motives...." Helmut Thielicke, the late German theologian and pastor compared prayer to making a phone call. He said sometimes we call God and only get a busy signal. He explained that while we think we are calling God we are really only dialing our own number so we get a busy signal. He says that we dial ourselves when we pray only for ourselves, only for the things we want. When our prayers deal only with our own self-concerns our prayers never go past the ceiling. We need to remember that God promised to meet all our needs not all our greeds.

The third explanation for unanswered prayers is requesting things God has already forbidden in his Word. For example, when my children were in high school, I told them they could not attend any party where alcohol was being served. Now, they could come back again and again and ask to go to a party and the answer would always be, "No." When God has said, "No," to something in his Word the answer will always be, "No."

The fourth explanation for unanswered prayer is asking when disobedient. The Bible tells us in 1st John 3:21–22, "Dear friends, if our hearts do not condemn us we have confidence before God and receive from him anything we ask because we obey his commands and do what pleases him."

The late Norman Vincent Peale tells about a time when, as a young boy, he was intrigued by smoking. One day he found a cigar so he went to an alley behind his house and lit up. He says the cigar did not taste very good but it made him feel grown-up. That is, until he saw his father enter the alley. Quickly Norman Vincent Peale put the cigar behind his back and tried to act casual. Desperately trying to divert his father's attention he pointed to a billboard at the corner advertising the circus coming to town. "Can we please go to the circus when it comes to town?" he asked.

Norman Vincent Peale says his father taught him a lesson he never forgot. "Son," his father answered quietly but firmly, "never make a petition while you're trying to hide the smoldering evidence of disobedience." How can we expect God to answer our prayers when we are living in disobedience and unconfessed sin?

Listen to what the Bible tells us in Isaiah 59:1–2, "Surely the arm of the Lord is not too short to save, nor his ear too dull to hear. But your iniquities have separated you from your God; your sins have hidden his face from you, so that he will not hear." And the Bible tells us in Proverbs 28:9, "If anyone turns a deaf ear to the law, even their prayers are detestable." While disobedience and unconfessed sin block our prayers, the Bible tells us in James 5:16, "The effective prayers of a righteous person can accomplish much."

About this time some of you may be thinking, I have been praying in faith. As far as I know my motives are right. I have not asked for things forbidden in God's Word. I am not aware of any unconfessed sin in my life. Still my prayers have not been answered. We have prayed for healing for sick family or friends. We have prayed for a job for an unemployed neighbor. We have prayed for financial support for missionaries, and no answers come. These are unselfish prayers made in faith. Where is God?

There is a fifth explanation for seemingly unanswered prayers. There was a young boy who desperately wanted a new bicycle for Christmas. Deep down he knew his parents could not afford it since his father was out of work but he kept hoping and praying. Every day he prayed for that bike. Christmas came and there was no bike only a few inexpensive gifts under the tree.

As the boy began to open his presents his father said, "Son I want you to know your mother and I are really sorry God didn't answer your prayers for a bicycle."

The boy turned to his father and said, "Oh, but God did answer my prayers, He said, 'No.'"

That is the fifth explanation: sometimes God says, "No." Sometimes God loves us so much he says, "No," when it is best for us. We have to trust God that he knows what is best for us. We find an example of this in the life of the Apostle Paul. In 2nd Corinthians 12:7–10, we read, ". . . there was given me a thorn in the flesh. . . . Three times I pleaded with the Lord to take it away from me. But he said to me, 'My grace is sufficient for you, for my power is made perfect in weakness.'"

What was Paul's response to this? He said, "Therefore I will boast more gladly about my weaknesses so that Christ's power may rest on me. That's why, for Christ's sake, I delight in weaknesses. . . . For when I am weak then I am strong." We need to trust God when he says, "No."

And then there is a sixth explanation: sometimes God says, "Not now." This was the case with Abraham and Sarah. They wanted a child and kept asking God and he kept saying, "Not now." Then finally they had Isaac. God's timing is the right timing; we need to leave it with him.

All this brings us to an illustration Jesus gives. In verses 9 to 11 he compares God to an earthly father. He argues that if earthly fathers know how to be good to their children, how much more does God know how to be good to his children? If we come to God in faith, with the right motives, and in obedience, God will always answer our prayers. Someone has said God has three answers to our requests: yes, no, and not now.

In Greek mythology Aurora, the goddess of dawn, fell in love with Tithonus, a mortal man. Zeus, the king of gods, gave her the privilege of choosing a gift for her mortal lover. Aurora asked that Tithonus be allowed to live forever. Her request was granted. However she never imagined the consequences of her request. Tithonus grew progressively older but he could never die. The gift became a curse.

We may ask for things from God, that from our limited human perspective look good and right, but God knows the beginning and the end. We should be just as ready to thank him when he says, "No," or, "Not now," as when he says, "Yes." In each instance he's given us his best for us.

That brings us to the result of our prayer life. In verse 12, we read, "So in everything do to others what you would have them do for you, for this sums up the law and the prophets." At first glance it is hard to see how this verse ties in with the preceding verses. The key word or clue is the word *so* (*Therefore* in other translations). This means, "as a result of what has just been said here is what you should do."

There are at least two things we should do as a result of God hearing and answering our prayers. First, because God does good for us we should do good for others. Second, because God loves us we should love others. The Bible tells us in Proverbs 21:13, "If someone shuts their ears to the cry of the poor, they too will cry out and not be answered." We should respond to others as we would want God to respond to us.

As we seek to apply what we have studied, let me leave you with four principles. First, we should come to God in faith, in obedience, and with proper motives. God is not a cosmic ATM machine that if we come with the proper PIN we can get what we want. God is the Creator of the Universe, the sovereign God, the Almighty. While he welcomes us as a Father, he expects us to come reverently and in accordance with his will.

Second, we must recognize that God sometimes says, "No." We have already looked at the example of the Apostle Paul. Let me show you another example from Scripture. You might want to get your Bible and to turn to the passage. It is Hebrews 11:32–40, where we read, "And what more shall I say? I do not have time to tell about Gideon, Barak, Samson, Jephthah, David, Samuel and the prophets who through faith conquered kingdoms, quenched the fury of the flames, and escaped the edge of the sword; whose weakness was turned to strength; who became powerful in battle and routed foreign armies. Women received back their dead, raised to life again."

All of this through the power of prayer, then in the middle of verse 35 we read, "Others were tortured and refused to be released so that they might gain a better resurrection. Some faced jeers and floggings, while still others were chained and put in prison. They were stoned, they were sawed in two; they were put to death by the sword. They went about in sheepskins and goatskins, destitute, persecuted, and mistreated. The world was not worthy of them. They wandered in deserts and mountains, in caves and holes in the ground."

Why were not their prayers answered, did they have less faith than those who were delivered? We find the answer in verses 39–40, "These were all commended for their faith yet none of them received what was promised. God had planned something better. . . ." We see things from the perspective of time; God sees things from the perspective of eternity. And that leads to the third principle: we must accept God's answers whether they are yes, no, or not now. We need to remember that God loves us and gives us his best even when we do not understand it.

The fourth principle is: we should give thanks for all things. The Bible tells us in 1 Thessalonians 5:18, "Give thanks in all circumstances for this is God's will for you in Christ Jesus." Why should we do that? The Bible tells us in Romans 8:28, "And we know that in all things God works for the good of those who love him, who have been called according to his purpose."

Now, this verse does not say all things are good. We live in a sin-ravaged world where horrible things happen. They happen to nonbelievers and believers alike. As believers we are not exempt from the ravages of sin. In fact sin is unfair, often those least deserving suffer the most. By the way, God is fair and just and sin is everything God is not. Sin is capricious and unfair. That is why the drunk driver walks away from the accident while a father of three lies dead in the street. That is why the wicked often seem to live in ease while the godly suffer.

By the way, if all that bothers you, read Psalm 73. For the first 15 verses the psalmist goes on and on about how unfair life is and how the wicked prosper. Then in verses 16 and 17 we read, "When I tried to understand all this it was oppressive to me until I entered the sanctuary of God; then I understood their final destiny." When you think life is unfair read Psalm 73 and Proverbs 24:19–20. What God promises us in Romans 8:28 is that, if we will let him, God can work for our good in the worst of circumstances. That is why we can give thanks in all circumstances. And we can bring everything to God in prayer.

11

How to Spot a Phony

Matthew 7:13–23

O<small>N</small> N<small>OVEMBER</small> 18<small>TH</small>, 1978, in a steamy jungle in Guyana, South
America, 913 Americans died in a suicide-murder ritual at a place
called Jonestown. Why would almost 1,000 Americans follow one man
to the jungles of South America? Why would most of them give cyanide-
laced kool-aid to their children and then drink it themselves? How did
Jonestown happen?

Jim Jones was raised in the small Indiana town of Lynn. While a
teenager he attended a Nazarene Church and made a profession of faith
in Christ. In the early 1950's he became pastor of a Methodist church in
Indianapolis. When he got into a dispute with the church leadership he left
the church and began to hold healing services in a rented building. This
grew into the People's Temple in Indianapolis. Soon Jones began preaching reincarnation and denying the virgin birth of Jesus. Then he began
to teach that the Bible was a black idol and accused fundamentalists of
worshipping it. He also began to emphasize social issues in his sermons.

In 1965 Jones and 150 of his followers moved from Indianapolis to
southern California. At that time he issued an ultimatum to his followers:
Choose me or Jesus. He told them, "You go out and preach Jim Jones and
I'll back it up with miracles." In a few years Jones had built the congregation of People's Temple to over 3,000 members.

Jones began to substitute his name for the name of Jesus in tradi-
tional hymns. He taught he was the reincarnation of Jesus and Buddha.
Jim Jones became obsessed with power. He demanded a 25% tithe from

his members as well as many hours of volunteer work each week. He demanded total loyalty from his followers and encouraged them to cut off outside relationships. In the early 1970's Jones predicted nuclear holocaust and lead his followers to Guyana to set up a utopian community. Jones' disciples not only followed him to Guyana, they followed him to their death.

Some 15 years later, on April 19th, 1993, in Waco, Texas, several dozen followers of David Koresh choose to burn to death in the Branch Davidian compound rather than surrender to Federal authorities. David Koresh had led his followers to believe that the compound was the ark of safety. Like Jones, David Koresh preached an approaching apocalypse.

Some four years later, followers of Marshall Applewhite, on March 26th, 1997, in Rancho Santa Fe, an upscale suburb of San Diego, committed suicide. Why did 39 members of the Heaven's Gate cult commit suicide? Applegate taught that they had to commit suicide so their souls could be taken by Jesus who was riding in a spaceship hiding behind the Comet Hale-Bopp.

How could thousands of people follow men like Jim Jones, David Koresh, and Marshall Applewhite to their death? To understand these tragedies we need to understand Jesus teaching in Matthew 7:13–23. Jim Jones, David Koresh, and Marshall Applewhite, are vivid illustrations of Jesus teaching in this passage.

By the way, members of these groups that did not participate in the suicides were interviewed and asked what attracted them to these groups. Their answers generally broke down into three categories. First was the lively music and dynamic preaching. Second was the warmth and acceptance. And third was the feeling of being part of something significant.

All of these are real needs, needs the true church should be meeting. People are hungry for a positive worship experience. People are lonely and hurting and looking for warmth and acceptance. And people want to be part of something bigger than themselves, something significant. What is larger and more significant than carrying out Jesus Christ's last command to bring the gospel to the world? To build the church of Jesus Christ and impact people for eternity?

False prophets are successful because they meet real needs. That is also why cults thrive, they meet real needs. Unfortunately they do not meet people's deepest need, having a relationship with God through faith in Jesus Christ. In Matthew 7:13–23 we learn what Jesus has to teach us about false prophets.

Jesus begins his discussion in verses 13 and 14 by pointing out there is a choice we must all make. Life is made up of choices and there are some decisions life forces us to make. Former Secretary of Labor, Raymond Donovan, tells about the first time he flew with President Reagan on Air Force One. He was seated right behind the President's cabin. At noon a steward came back and said to him, "Mr. Secretary, the President would like you to join him for lunch."

As Donovan entered the President's cabin a red phone on his desk rang. President Reagan waved Donovan to sit down as he answered the red phone. As Donovan sat, President Reagan said gravely into the phone, "I see, I see, I understand." Then he paused to listen and finally asked, "Well then, what are my options?"

"Oh my goodness," thought Donovan, "I'm here while history is being made." Meanwhile President Reagan listened again and then said, "Well, alright, then I'll have the ice tea." Some choices, like that faced by President Reagan on that flight, are not very momentous. Other choices are literally life and death decisions.

Many years ago, during a turbulent war in the Middle East, a spy was captured and sentenced to death by a general in the Persian army. The general, a man of intelligence and humanity, had developed an interesting and unusual custom. He permitted condemned prisoners to make a choice. The prisoner could either face a firing squad or pass through a black door.

The condemned spy was asked, "What shall it be? The black door or the firing squad?" This was not an easy choice, the prisoner hesitated. Then he announced he preferred the firing squad to the unknown horrors behind the black door. A few minutes later a volley of shots were heard in the courtyard.

The general, starring at his boots said to his aide, "You see how it is with men. They will usually choose the known way to the unknown. I gave the prisoner a choice, the firing squad was his decision." The aide, who was new to his position, asked the general what lay behind the black door. "Freedom," replied the general, "And I've only known a few men brave enough to choose it."

In Matthew 7:13–14 Jesus talks about a choice we must all make involving two ways. The first way is the broad way that leads to destruction.

In verse 13 Jesus points out that the wide gate is easy to enter and the broad way is easy to follow. It is popular, it is the way the crowd is going, so it must be the right way. But Jesus says it leads to destruction.

The second way is the narrow way that leads to life. In verse 14 Jesus talks about a small gate and a narrow way. In the original language the connotation is that it is just wide enough for one person at a time to pass through. The idea is not that there is limited access but that it is a personal decision, an individual decision.

Jesus says this narrow way leads to life. It is interesting to note that he does not say "eternal life." Christianity is more than pie-in-the-sky-by-and-by, it is abundant life here and now. In John 10:10 Jesus declared that he had come so we might have life and have it more abundantly.

By the way, in the Bible, people without Christ are called spiritu-ally dead while people with Christ are spiritually alive. People without Christ are literally the walking dead. For believers, eternal life does not begin when we die, it begins the moment we receive Christ into our lives. Spiritual life is living in fellowship with God while spiritual death is be-ing separated from God. And when we die the spiritually alive will spend eternity with God while the spiritually dead with be eternally separated from God. We face a choice, each of us must choose the path we will fol-low. Will it be the broad, popular path that leads to destruction or the narrow path that leads to life?

In the Canadian Rockies is a stream called Divide Creek. At a point in its course the creek divides at a large boulder. Waters that flow west of the boulder rush into Kicking Horse River and eventually into the Pacific Ocean. Waters flowing east of the boulder run into the Bow River and eventually into the Atlantic Ocean. Once the waters divide at the boulder their eventual destiny is sealed.

In the Bible Jesus Christ is compared to a rock. When we encounter him we make a decision that determines our eternal destiny. There are many false prophets that would lead us astray. They would lead us down the broad path to destruction. How do we recognize false prophets?

In verses 15–20 Jesus warns us against false prophets and gives us a test for detecting them. A prophet is someone who claims to speak for God or claims to speak God's Word. Therefore a false prophet is one who claims to speak for God but really does not. He claims to offer the way of life but actually offers the way of destruction.

The Bible compares believers to sheep and Christ as the Shepherd. Wolves are natural enemies of sheep. Jesus teaches us that these false prophets are wolves in sheep's clothing. In other words, outwardly they give the appearance of being believers but underneath they are really our enemies. Jesus goes on to tell us we can spot them by their fruit.

Several years ago when I was teaching at St. Paul Bible College, now Crown College, we had a garden plot at the college. There were a few acres behind the college that they tilled and allowed faculty and staff to stake out plots. We gave our two youngest children, Becki and Jaime, who were in grade school at the time, some seeds to plant.

They planted their seeds but forgot what they planted where. We had no idea what was planted in some rows. We had to wait to see what came up to see what had been planted. Each seed did produce after its kind. Lettuce seeds produced lettuce and cucumber seeds produced cucumbers. The Bible tells us in Galatians 6:6, "Do not be deceived, whatever people sow that will they reap."

Let me share four fruit or signs of a false prophet. First, anyone who promotes himself or herself rather than Jesus Christ is a false prophet. The calling of all believers is to point people to Christ. John the Baptist said, "He must increase but I must decrease." The Apostle Paul declared, "For I have determined to know nothing among you except Jesus Christ." And the Apostle John wrote, "We bear witness to and proclaim the Word of Life [Jesus Christ]."

We saw how Jim Jones replaced Jesus' name with his name in hymns. Now most false prophets are not that blatant. But as you observe TV ministries, religious leaders, and lay people, see who they are lifting up, themselves or Jesus? Do they talk about what they have done or what Jesus is doing?

A second sign is anyone who denies the Bible as the Word of God is a false prophet. Now, we are not worshippers of the Bible, we are worshippers of the God of the Bible. However we do believe that God has revealed himself to us through his Word. News accounts report that Jim Jones denounced the Bible as unreliable and disavowed its moral standards. So did David Koresh. We have learned from followers who left the compound before the fire that he engaged in immoral behavior with his followers including children.

Again, most false prophets are not that blatant, at least in public. But they undermine the authority of the Bible with their teaching. They elevate human experience and their ideas above the Bible. Beware of any ministry that places human experience or other ideas above the Bible. Now, they will not say they are doing that. In fact they will claim they follow the Bible. But, do they judge their experiences and ideas in light of Scripture or do they use the Bible to support their experiences and ideas?

A third sign is anyone who teaches salvation by any means other than faith in Jesus Christ is a false prophet. The Apostle Paul wrote in Galatians 1:8 "If we, or an angel from heaven should preach to you a gospel contrary to that which we have preached, let him be a eternally condemned."

What gospel did Paul preach? We find it in 1 Corinthians 15:1,3,4, where we read, "I want to remind you of the gospel I preached to you. . . . For what I received I passed on to you . . . that Christ died for our sins according to the Scriptures, that he was buried, that he was raised on the third day according to the Scriptures." And in Ephesians 2:8–9, he wrote, "For it is by grace you have been saved, through faith—and this not of yourselves, it is the gift of God—not by works that no one can boast." Anyone who adds or takes away from that message is a false prophet.

There are two errors prevalent today. One is universalism. This is the view that everyone is saved, that everyone will end up in heaven. People who hold this view define evangelism as bringing people the good news that they are saved. However, the only thing universal about the gospel is that Jesus Christ died for the sins of everyone and salvation is available to everyone through faith in Jesus Christ. Each person must make their own personal choice.

Back in 1830 a man named George Wilson was arrested and tried for robbing the US mail. He was convicted and sentenced to be hanged. Because of extenuating circumstances President Andrew Jackson signed a pardon for Wilson. However George Wilson refused to accept the pardon. The case went all the way to the Supreme Court where Chief Justice Marshall ruled Wilson would have to hang. In his opinion Justice Marshall wrote, "A pardon is a slip of paper the value of which is determined by acceptance of the person pardoned." And so it is with Christ's death for our sins; we're only pardoned if we accept his death for us by faith. Each of us faces a choice, the broad way or the narrow way.

The second error that is prevalent today is legalism. This view says we have to do something to be saved. In its more popular forms legalism says we have to be baptized, or join the church, or do good deeds to be saved. Now all these things are good and important but they do not save. Good works are a sign of salvation and the result of salvation, not the means of salvation. We are not saved by being good, we are saved to be good. As someone has said, "Sitting in a garage and drinking gasoline won't make you a car and sitting in church and going through the rituals won't make you a Christian." By the way, this is what separates true Christianity from all other religions. In other religions you earn your salvation, in true Christianity you receive it by faith.

The fourth sign is anyone who panders to our selfish and sinful desires is a false prophet. The Bible tells us in 2 Timothy 3:2–5: "For people will be lovers of self, lovers of money, boastful, arrogant, revilers . . . conceited, lovers of pleasure rather than lovers of God; holding to a form of godliness although they have denied its power; avoid such people as these. . . ."

And in 2 Peter 2:1–3 the Bible tells us, "False prophets also arose among the people just as there will be false prophets among you, who will secretly introduce destructive heresies even denying the Master who bought them. . . . especially those who indulge the flesh in its corrupt desires. . . having eyes full of adultery and that never cease from sin; enticing unstable souls, having a heart trained in greed, accursed children; forsaking the right way they have gone astray."

I would personally be suspicious of any ministry that promised health, wealth, and happiness. Any ministry that emphasizes the satisfaction of our worldly desires and panders to our selfishness is not of God. The Bible calls for commitment and sacrifice on the part of Jesus' disciples. It promises persecution and rejection to those who are faithful to the gospel. The Bible calls for giving ourselves and our resources for the cause of Christ. Now, it is true that God promises joy, peace, and contentment to the followers of Christ. But it is not based on possessions and position, it is based on our relationship with him. Our citizenship is in heaven, any ministry that emphasizes the values of this world is not of God.

Then in verses 21–23 Jesus goes on to discuss the judgment of false prophets and those who follow the broad way. In verse 21 Jesus talks about profession without possession. There are those who claim to be followers of Jesus, who, in fact, are not. Jesus makes three points in these verses. The first is, it is not those who claim to be Jesus' followers that truly are, but those who obey him. We find the second point in verse 22, ministry done in Jesus' name is not always his ministry. There were apparently people healed in some of Jim Jones' services.

Back in the Old Testament book of Exodus, the false prophets of Egypt also did miracles. As believers we need to be alert and discerning. Just because a person claims to be a minister of Jesus Christ, just because there appear to be miracles, does not mean it is of God. The Bible teaches that Satan himself appears as an angel of light. The Bible tells us to test the spirits and examine the fruit.

Then in verse 23 Jesus tells us the final end of false prophets and those who follow the broad way. That is Jesus' third point, false prophets and those who follow the broad road will be eternally cut off from God.

We need to apply the truths we have learned. We will use three questions to help us do that. The first question is: have I decided to choose Jesus? Am I on the broad way or the narrow way? Again, the narrow way is not narrow because it is exclusive, it is narrow because it is personal and individual. It is available to all but it is a personal choice.

If you have never made that choice you can do it right now. Just reach out to God and confess that you have sinned, that you have violated his commands. He gave those commands to guide and protect us not restrict and limit us. They were given to set us free. Ask God to forgive you because Jesus died for your sins. Then invite him into your life.

The second question is, am I testing the spirits? As believers we need to practice discernment when it comes to ministries and religious leaders both nationally and in the local church. False teachers and false believers do not go after the lost, they go after believers. We need to be alert.

The third question is, am I ready for the judgment? Perhaps one of the most ironic touches to Jonestown was that hanging just above the seat from which Jim Jones ordered the mass suicide-murders was a sign that read: "Those who do not remember the past are condemned to repeat it."

12

Which Are You?

Matthew 7:24–29

"IT WAS THE BEST of times, it was the worst of times." While those words could describe our day, they are the opening words of Charles Dickens classic novel about the French revolution, *A Tale of Two Cities*. The two cities Dickens wrote about were London and Paris. I would like to tell you about two other cities. London and Paris are in the Old World, the two I want to tell about are in the New World.

The first city is New York, home to some of the tallest buildings in the world. In fact, of the 100 tallest building in the world, 20% of them are found in New York City. For example, the tallest building in Kansas City, Missouri, is One Kansas City Place, it is some 42 stories tall. New York City has well over a dozen buildings that would tower over One Kansas City Place including: the Empire State Building at 102 stories, the Chrysler Building at 77 stories, and the Pan AM Building at 59 stories. Manhattan Island is able to support so many large buildings because the island is a solid rock which forms a strong foundation for these gigantic structures.

The second city I want to look at is one of the largest cities in the world with a population of over 14 million people. This is also a beautiful city with many large buildings. Mexico City is built on a high plateau; it is also built on a lake. Mexico City was originally an island in Lake Texcoco. The Spanish filled in the lake so they could expand the city. The soil under Mexico City is 85% water. The national Palace, built in the 1600's is a beautiful, marble structure. It has sunk 15 feet into the soggy soil since it was built. According to news reports, some buildings in Mexico City are sinking at a rate of 12 inches a year. A story of two cities, one built on solid rock, able to support some of the largest buildings in the world, the other built on a filled in lake and sinking

Jesus closes the Sermon on the Mount with a story about two men who built their houses on two different foundations. It is interesting that Jesus does not distinguish between the houses the men built. They were probably very similar in design and appearance. They were very likely constructed from the same materials. Outwardly they would have been difficult to tell apart. Both houses were subjected to the same trials and storms. One house survived, the other did not. The reason one house survived and the other did not had nothing to do with their design, building materials, or construction, it had everything to do with their foundations.

Some years ago Josh McDowell came out with a book titled *More Than a Carpenter*. His thesis was that Jesus was more than a carpenter, he was the Son of God. Without realizing it, Josh McDowell's title had more truth than he realized. We have all seen pictures of Jesus, as a boy, helping his father, Joseph, in the carpenter's shop. But, was Joseph a carpenter and did Jesus learn carpentry?

The word *carpenter* is used two times in our English New Testaments. The first use is in Matthew 13:55 where Jesus is called the carpenter's son. The second is in Mark 6:3 where Jesus is called a carpenter. But, as you know, the New Testament was not written in English, it was written in Greek. The same Greek word, *tekton*, is used in both passages and it means a builder. The fact is, in all likelihood, Joseph was a home builder and that was the trade Jesus learned. Some of the early church fathers also allude to this.

Since homes in England were made of wood, when the English translators came to the word *tekton*, they translated it *carpenter*. Jesus never used any carpentry illustrations but he did use home-building illustrations. The point is, Jesus knew about building homes. He understood that the most critical part of a house is the foundation.

When we lived in Minnesota we had a vacant lot next door to our home. A young couple purchased the lot and decided to have a prefabricated home put on it. In northern states you have to build the foundation below the frost line. Since the frost can go down as far as 5 feet you have to dig down at least 6 feet. The once you have dug that deep you might as well as put in a basement.

So this couple had a basement dug and the foundation poured. Then the manufacturer delivered the prefabricated home on a series of huge flatbed trailers. Each wall was fully built with wiring, plumbing, and whatever else that was needed including windows. It was like putting a kit together. In one day the whole house was up.

However, there was a problem. The house hung over the foundation by a couple of inches on one corner. When the building inspector came he would not approve the house. The house sat empty for a couple of years as the lawsuits flew back and forth. The building inspector would not allow the house to be approved without a solid foundation. What kind of foundation are we building our lives on? In Matthew 7:24–29, we find the foundations used by the foolish builder and the wise builder.

In verses 24–25 Jesus tells us two things about the wise builder. First, he tells us, the wise builder is the one who hears and obeys Jesus. In Luke 11:28, Jesus taught, "Blessed . . . are those who hear the Word of God and obey it." In John 13:17, he said, "Now that you know these things you will be blessed if you do them." And the Bible tells us in Revelation 1:3, "Blessed is the one who reads the words of this prophecy, and blessed are those who hear it and take to heart what is written in it. . . ." There is no blessing in just knowing God's Word, it is the knowing and obeying that brings blessing.

Second, Jesus tells us the person is wise because his words are true and they work. What the Bible teaches is not only true, it is functional, it works. God loves us, knows what is best for us, and wants the best for us; his commands are for our good, we benefit when we obey.

Those of you who follow sports know that the former Atlanta Falcons' star quarterback, Michael Vick, was suspended from football and arrested on dog fighting charges. He was found guilty and sentenced to prison. Not only was he suspended from football and sent to prison he lost a number of lucrative endorsement contracts. Here is a man of tremendous physical talent. A man with so much to gain. But he decided he knew better. He chose to ignore God's instructions.

However, it is not just football players and famous people who lose when they go their own way, it is all of us, it is me and you. We think we are smarter than God. Oh, we would never say that, at least in words, but we say it in actions every time we disobey him. When we disobey, we are saying to God, in this instance I know better than you what is best for me. And we may get away with it for a while, but in the long run we lose. God does not want us to be losers, he wants us to be winners, and when we do it his way, we win. That is why the wise builder builds his or her life on the foundation of God's Word.

Next Jesus describes the foolish builder. In verses 26–27 he points out the foolish builder builds his or her life on an unstable foundation. What are some unstable foundations on which people build their lives? There are several unstable foundations that are quite prevalent in our culture. One is possessions.

One of things my wife, Sandy, and I liked about living in San Diego for eight years was being by the ocean. Both of us grew up in the New York City area and lived near the ocean. For the first 12 years of my life I lived three blocks from the ocean. The first year Sandy and I were married we lived half-a-block from the ocean. We have spent a lot of time by the sea. One of things I enjoy is watching children play in the sand by the ocean.

One time I was watching some children playing on the beach. They were building sand castles. They seemed so intent on their project. It was interesting to watch how meticulously they worked the crumbly sand. Then a big wave started to close in on their project. But the children did not panic, rather they did a strange thing. They jumped to their feet and screamed with excitement as the wave washed away their creation. There was no panic, no sadness, no bitterness. They were not surprised or angry. They realized that when they built their sand castles by the sea the waves would come and wash them away.

You and I could learn a lot from those children. You see, we also build sand castles. Oh, we call them bank accounts, stock portfolios, retirement accounts, homes, cars, and other possessions. But they are sand castles and the waves of time will eventually wash them away, and in some cases, much sooner than we expect.

Rudyard Kipling, speaking to the graduating class of McGill University in Montreal, Canada, years ago, said: "If a person's scale of values is based solely on material wealth that person will be in difficulty all of his or her life. Do not pay too much attention to . . . money. Some day you will meet a person who cares for none of [it] and then you will know how poor you really are."

Now, there is nothing wrong with money and possessions. They can be used to accomplish a lot of good including caring for and raising our families, supporting God's work, and helping others. I have possessions, all of us have possessions, but we need to be careful we are not building our lives on them.

You see, when we build our lives on money and stuff, we do not possess them, they possess us. Jesus taught that no one can serve two masters; we will serve either God or possessions. When we build our lives on money and possessions they become our master. Money and possessions are a stewardship; they are to be used, but not to build our lives on. We need to enjoy what God has provided but hold on to what we have very loosely.

A second unstable foundation is power. Power can be very addictive. Someone has said, "Power corrupts and absolute power corrupts absolutely." Now there is a difference between power and leadership. Power is using others for our benefit. Leadership is guiding others for their benefit.

The Bible is the story of leaders from Joseph to Moses to Joshua to the judges to the kings to the prophets to the apostles. Jesus trained his disciples to be leaders. But what he taught was servant leadership. History is replete with the accounts of people who tried to build their lives on power. And the foundation crumbled.

A third unstable foundation is position. Many people want a title and a position along with the prestige and privileges that go with it. They want all the benefits of the position. But few people want to accept the responsibilities that go with it. Positions are unstable foundations because they can easily be lost. Politicians lose elections, executives get fired, and fame can be fickle.

Now, there is nothing wrong with having a position. Many of us have one. The issue is, is it our identity? Is it the foundation on which we are building our lives? Or is our position a platform for serving others and serving God? When God allows us to hold a position we need to see it as a trust and an opportunity.

The fourth unstable foundation is pleasure. Pleasure is based on circumstances and circumstances change. Again, there is nothing wrong with pleasure that comes from the right things. God gives us many good things to enjoy. However pleasure is not a foundation on which to build a life. King Solomon, in the Old Testament, tried to build his life on pleasure and in Ecclesiastes, chapter 2, he said it was meaningless.

There is one more unstable foundation people build their lives on. In some ways this is the most unstable foundation of all. It is religion. What makes religion so unstable is that it gives false hope. It teaches us to trust in creeds, in rituals, in church membership, in good works, in everything and anything except God. Now, some of you may thinking, but are not those all things God's interested in? No, God is interested in us and wants to have a personal relationship with us. God is not interested in religion; he is interested in a relationship with us based on faith in his Son, Jesus Christ.

"Well," you ask, "if we are not to build our lives on religion, what are we to build our lives on?" The true builder. Who is the true builder? The true builder is Jesus Christ. The Bible tells us in 1 Corinthians 3:11, "For no one can lay any foundation other than the one already laid, which is Jesus Christ."

The Bible also tells us that Jesus Christ is the cornerstone. The Bible tells us in 1 Peter 2:4–6, "As you come to [Jesus Christ], the living stone . . . you also like living stones are being built into a spiritual house. . . . For in Scripture it says: 'See, I lay in Zion, a chosen and precious cornerstone, and the one who trusts in him will never be put to shame.'"

Then in Matthew 7:28–29, we read, "When Jesus had finished saying these things, the crowds were amazed at his teaching, because he taught as one who had authority, and not as their teachers of the law." Jesus Christ spoke with the authority of God because he was God incarnate. Our authority comes from the Word of God.

By way of application we will look at three ways to build our lives on Jesus Christ. The first way is by faith. Trusting in possessions, power, position, pleasure, and even religion is basically trusting in ourselves. It is trusting in what we have, what we have accomplished, what we can do. And the Bible clearly teaches that anything and everything we are, have, or can do falls short. All of it is an unstable foundation that the sands of time will wash away. The only solid foundation on which to build our lives is Jesus Christ. And the only way we do that is by faith. If you have never put your life on the foundation of Jesus by faith, I would like to invite you to do that now.

To build your life on the foundation of Jesus Christ, all you have to do is reach out to God by faith. We do this by admitting we have sinned, that is, we have tried to run our lives our way instead of God's way. We ask God to forgive us because Jesus died for our sins, he paid the penalty. And we invite God into our lives. It is my prayer, that if you have never done this, you will do it now.

The second way to build our lives on the foundation of Jesus Christ is by obedience. The Bible tells us in 1st Corinthians 3:11–15, "For no can lay any foundation other than the one already laid, which is Jesus Christ. If anyone builds on this foundation using gold, silver, costly stones, wood, hay or straw, their work will be shown for what it is. . . . It will be revealed with fire, and the fire will test the quality of each one's work. If what they have built survives they will receive their reward. If it is burned up, they will suffer lose; they themselves will be saved, but only as one escaping through flames."

Let me show you an interesting passage of Scripture. It is Revelation 19:6–8 which reads, "Hallelujah! Our Lord God Almighty reigns. Let us rejoice and be glad and give him glory! For the wedding of the Lamb has come, and his bride has made herself ready. Fine linen, bright and clean, was given her to wear. Fine linen stands for the righteous acts of the saints."

In the Bible *saints* does not refer to late great Christians, it refers to all believers. In the Bible all believers are referred to as saints. And Revelation 19:8 says the fine linen stands for our righteous acts. Let me ask a question: will there be enough linen for us to be properly dressed?

While Ephesians 2:8–9 clearly teaches that we are saved by faith not by works, verse 10 goes on to say, "For we are God's workmanship, created in Christ Jesus to do good works, which God prepared in advance for us to do." We are not saved by good works we are saved to do good works. We build on the foundation by obedience.

The third way we build our lives on the foundation of Jesus Christ is by sharing. The last command Jesus left us was to share our faith with others. Jesus said we were to be his witnesses. In fact, Jesus' last command was for us to take the gospel everywhere. We have a message people need and we need to share it.

In these chapters we have looked together at the Sermon on the Mount, Jesus' climbing instructions for his followers. It is my prayer that these studies will help all of us climb with Jesus and to become committed disciples of our Lord and Savior. Jesus invites us to join him in the great adventure of building his kingdom.